Project/Program Management

LEADERSHIP
SPIRIT

A Collection of Leadership Applications

For

PRACTICING LEADERS, PROJECT AND PROGRAM MANAGERS

Steven L. Wilson, PMP

Copyright © 2009 by Steven L. Wilson
LEADERSHIP *SPIRIT*
by Steven Wilson
ISBN: 978-0-557-17138-5

All rights reserved solely by the author. The author guarantees all contents are the original and do not infringe upon the legal rights of any other person or work. No part of this book may be reproduced in any form without the permission of the author.

LEADERSHIP

SPIRIT

LEADERSHIP
SPIRIT
Is dedicated to
My loving wife
Laura

Laura, I love you more than words can describe. Many have heard me say I am a better man for being married to you. You mean everything to me. Our years together have been off-the-charts special. Your kindness, caring and unconditional love overwhelms me. You have supported me through this project, and truth be told your encouragement brought me to the end of this project with confidence even on my most desperate and challenging days. I appreciate you reading through every word, several times, feeding my passion and taking on the thankless job of "first look" editing. Most of all I have appreciated you being my chief encourager. Thank you for being in my life and all you bring to my life. You are God's special blessing and His gift to me...143.

Forever Yours,

Steven

Special Thanks To

Rhonda Pope

Rhonda, you are a great friend! You may remember the four of us sitting in our living room and me asking you to take on the task of a researcher for this book project. I remember you graciously accepting and wanting nothing in return, knowing the huge time commitment you would need to make. After seven months of your hard work our book is complete, and because of *your* work the message this book brings to its readers will have a more significant impact because of you. I am so grateful and I want to thank you for your selfless commitment and dedication to this project, but most of all thanks for your friendship over these years.

Respectfully,

Steven

Praise for LEADERSHIP SPIRIT

Tony Johnson, MBA, PMP, PgMP

CEO & Founder, Crosswind Project Management Inc.

"Leadership Sprit is an invigorating book that allows you to jump in and see examples and perspectives that can be immediately applied to our professional and personal life. Leadership is not just a given, and the numerous professional and scriptural examples help show various perspectives on how to be a better leader and person. The direct application to project and program management can also be a great help to those that are challenged in growing their project and program management skills."

Tamara B. Burris, PMP, BB

EPMO Organizational Effectiveness Manager, Xerox Corporation

"Steve Wilson has provided a holistic approach to exploring the attributes of good leadership as it relates to program and project management that is both innovative and captivating. With a conversational writing style that is easy to read and a sense of humor that keeps you entertained, Steve shares his passion for the profession and provides pearls of wisdom that may inspire growth in one's personal or professional life. Steve leaves the reader contemplating the 'leadership spirit' in all of us!"

Kieran Wright, PMP, Certified Hypnotist

EMEA Business Development, PgO Lead, Strategic Governance Lead, Risk Champion, EDS an HP Company

"In an entirely fresh take on the genre, Steve imparts his nuggets of wisdom with the honesty and candor of an old friend. Some of the situations Steve describes will resonate so deeply that you'll find yourself responding by either laughing out loud, cringing, or just plain marveling at the insight he shows. His unique writing style is peppered with humor which is guaranteed to hold your attention, but he also has the rare ability to 'tell it like it is'. What comes across most clearly though, is his earnest desire to ensure that everyone takes something away in terms of personal growth."

Tony Pottle

CEO & Founder, Time to Be Great Consulting, LLC

"Steve's vast project management experience and wisdom comes across loud and clear! The Biblical principles in Leadership Spirit and the practical application examples give me great confidence anyone will succeed using this book."

Andrew Lacy, PMP

Senior Project Manager

"Leadership SPIRIT provided me with guidance on leadership based on real world experience that is applicable both at work and home. Leadership SPIRIT was very enjoyable to read and provided excellent advice. I especially enjoyed the enthusiasm, passion and positive message of Leadership SPIRIT. Congratulations on your book and the next chapter of your journey."

Jon Stephens

Spiritual Formation Pastor, Crosswinds Wesleyan Church

"Leadership SPIRIT is one of the most holistic books on leadership I have ever read. It contains an enormous wealth of wisdom for leaders of all experience levels in all types of leadership settings. Steve writes with the voice of a mentor, a coach, and a friend. I would enthusiastically recommend it to my peers in all positions of leadership."

CONTENTS

Introduction 11
Preface 13
Chapter 1: Leadership 17
    Winds of Change 18
    The Perfect Storm 20
    When All is Said and Done...You Make the Call 22
    Keep Your Vision Clear 24
    It's a Pressure Cooker 26
    Enthusiastically Yours 28
    Build a "Leadership Circle" 30
    Turn Your Back to the Crowd 32
    Mucus Trooper 34
    Cheer for the Underdog 36
    Knowledge Yields Respect 38
    Make Your Meetings Memorable 40
    Influence and Direction 42
    Don't Cower 44

Chapter 2: Humility 49
    Confidence vs. Arrogance...It's a Fine Line 50
    The Ego Meter 52
    Proud Not Prideful 54
    Don't Doubt the Benefit 56
    The Blessing of Success 58

Chapter 3: Spiritual Wisdom 61
    Live and Learn 62
    Big Ears 64
    Wisdom For Free 66

Purest Wisdom 68
Right is Always Right.. 70

Chapter 4: Communication.................................. 73
Get in Front of Your Communication 74
The 800-Pound Gorilla 76
The Fifteen-Minute Meeting 78

Chapter 5: Balance... 81
The Teeter Tauter 82
Pace Yourself for the Long Haul............................ 84
Start-up is Nothing Short of Critical 86
Cheat Your Employer... 88
What Color is Your Flag? 90

Chapter 6: Character.. 93
Gloom and Doomer.. 94
Right or Privilege?... 96
Have Their Back 98
Less is More... 100
Resist and Run 102
Kill Them with Kindness..................................... 104
Truth and Consequences.................................... 106
Old Dog New Tricks... 108

Chapter 7: Relationships 111
Never Burn a Bridge.. 112
The Iceberg Theory 114
Office Cliques 116
The Core of Success.. 118

Chapter 8: Excellence... 121
Liar-ship? 122
Bring Our Best to Bear...................................... 124
Execute 126

    Add Value Every Day..128

    Finish Well..130

Chapter 9: Rewards and Recognition 133

    Working With Passion.......................................134

    A Blind Eye..136

    Whole = Sum of its Parts..................................138

Chapter 10: Growth.. 141

    Professional Growth 142

    Re-Invent Yourself..144

    Learning While You Lead..................................146

    Success To Significance...................................148

    Annual Physical 150

Quote References.. 157

Bible References 165

About the Author 173

Introduction

A couple of years ago, I celebrated what could be called "halftime", my fiftieth birthday, and it prompted more positive reflection than I had ever anticipated. I found myself digging deep to examine and reflect on my experiences as a leader. As a practicing project management professional, teacher, mentor and coach I had a desire to give back, share and pass on my most valuable lessons learned over the past twenty years.

Please, make no mistake, I don't mean to imply that I have "graduated", as I will always desire to be a student, striving to grow, when it comes to leadership learning. In fact, I believe we all must learn while we lead.

My purpose in writing this book, and I believe my responsibility as a leader, is to share some experiences and concepts that have strengthened me through the years in the hopes that what I have learned will benefit you and others.

This book is for leaders, project/program leaders, contributors and those of us working hard to become better human beings. A word of caution, although I dig in on some project/program situations, this is not a book about the "how to" in-depth concepts of the project management discipline. The principles in this book will help you glean leadership applications around the project and program management. It is also my sincere hope that it will help you to grow in your wisdom and faith.

Leadership SPIRIT provides lessons that explore different topics relating to leadership, wisdom, character, humility, relationships, balance, communication, excellence, rewards and recognition, and growth. Each lesson begins with a title, an applied quote, a view on the lesson subject, followed by a relevant verse from the Bible. The next facing page concludes the lesson with a related project/program management application to include practical insights, suggestions, and a few provocative questions to encourage you along your journey.

This book is designed to be read over time maybe one lesson per day or even one each week, it is up to you to decide. The lessons are not

Introduction

dated in any way, so you can start anywhere you please. Don't worry about reading the book from front to back, as it is not designed in a linear fashion. Skip around if you like, but keep in mind that if you consistently spend fifteen minutes a day reading it, I can promise, you will be on your way toward a lifelong habit of growing your leadership skills.

I would strongly encourage you to journal, especially if the lesson raises confusion, a challenge or an application in your life or work. Journaling can be helpful by writing your thoughts in the margin or on paper then making reference to it in the future. Most of all, put into practice the practical tips and application you learn in your own life and/or work scenarios.

I know you are busy and at times under stress. That is why this book is designed in such a way that each lesson offers helpful information and insights in short order. As you read, I hope you will reflect on the lesson, quotes and relevant passages and consider how they apply to your life in and outside of your job.

Regardless of our role in the project management space, everyone in some capacity is a leader. It is my desire, hope and prayer that *Leadership SPIRIT* will help you become a more effective leader so you can help someone else along their journey.

Preface

The project/program management discipline continues to grow and is recognized globally as a qualified discipline that links directly to a company's bottom line through operational and organizational efficiencies.

Experience tells me that today's project team needs a different type of leader than our command and control cultures from the past. They need leaders who will help them shine, who help them fulfill their potential, leaders who improve their thinking. Best-selling author Jim Collins, said it this way: "True leadership only exists if people follow when they have the freedom not to."

Our project/program leadership is unlike any other. We have all had delicate days with those project moments where things just seem to be a crazy. We may even ask ourselves at one time or another, "Am I fully capable?" Or we might have had a morning when we woke up and sat on the edge of our bed thinking, "Can I make it another day leading the charge?"

Leadership and project leadership is really a call to action. As leaders we have a huge responsibility, and we all know we can't take it lightly. Part of the responsibility is our own values in relation to growing as a leader, or a project/program leader. As a leader, we crave new information, strategies and new experiences to grow. Have we settled on our professional and, more importantly, personal values that no matter what, we will *not* compromise?

We have chosen to develop and execute strategies, to push the vision, to be the example, meet our objectives and our deliverables, develop partnerships, and be an extraordinary negotiator. We must have the highest level of integrity, build trust, manage conflict, champion high morale and deliver employee satisfaction in this challenging, ever-changing world. Truth be told, as leaders we are psychiatrists, psychologists, moms, dads, and even sometimes I bet we feel like wardens. We have the responsibility to build and develop our own leadership capability and maintain both our personal and professional values.

PREFACE

It's funny, project/program leaders do not sit in the back seat — we can't. We want to drive — we need to drive. In fact, we do not want to just drive, we want to get there and finish well. We want to make a difference to our teams, those around us, and to our organizations. We have chosen to lead!

I'll bet we all have stories where we were wondering how we could find the endurance to face one more day, even one more hour. Well, we did and here we are. The good news is we can all share dozens of stories to indicate the best times, successes and leadership victories as we represent our profession proudly and proficiently.

What sets us apart is we value serving people, developing trust and bringing our teams along to function at their full unified and spirited capacity. Not operating as silos or islands but cohesive and cooperative units. Most importantly, we do it with excellence, and it starts with cornerstone values of integrity, trust and unwavering high ethical principles that cannot be compromised — we remain unshaken, solid and unbendable. We can't and we won't settle for anything less. In fact, it almost needs to be our obsession. We must be in the sweet spot, the bull's-eye of the integrity target, and the highest ethical target right in the center of the project target with our teams — everything based on trust. There must never be a question of where we stand on these values, no question at all. Without this, the rest means nothing because we have built our values on sinking sand with no foundation. We will lose our integrity, our leadership, the team could be negatively labeled, and those that need to believe in us will not.

This book is an opportunity for me to serve you. What excites me is that you have selected this book to build into yourself so you can build into others. This is what leadership discipline is... serving others.

Even if you take only one nugget of wisdom from this book to strengthen your leadership or to serve your team in whatever capacity or industry you are in, my hope and my prayer is that this book will serve you well.

Several years ago, I received a card from an executive leader. We had the opportunity to get to know each other well over time and he was a master at recognizing and acknowledging his employees. When I received his card I was not only touched by his gesture, but it was the words he selected that cut deep into me and continues to impact my leadership. He said: *"The measure of a true leader is how many people you carry forward, not how far and fast you go."*

Thank you to the many leaders who have coached me along my journey. I thank my many teams who have challenged me over the years, but most of all I thank my God, who inspires me through His timeless teachings.

Steven

Chapter 1

Leadership

Winds of Change

Leadership

"The one unchangeable certainly is that nothing is unchangeable or certain."

— John F. Kennedy

Changes in life. Organizational rapid change. Everyone, including our kids, is making big, life changes and decisions that impact the trajectory of their lives — who they will marry, career path, what college/university they will attend, where they will live, etc. Many of us are making changes to care for aging parents along with managing our own health issues. In almost all aspects of life, we find ourselves asking: "Whatever happened to normal?" What was once a routine day seems to have turned into something more like confusion and chaos. I'll bet recently, all of us in some capacity have been through a real change — or we are about to. Of late, I have been speaking with many people suffering the consequences of our recent recession. Many are working through unemployment challenges. They are experienced, qualified, men and women and they want to contribute and work hard. My eldest son left a couple of years ago for LA to pursue his dream job. Now my youngest son is chasing his dream to work in law enforcement on the southeast coast. My wife's parents are in their mid-eighties and their health is failing significantly. Change, change and more change, and I doubt your life is any different than mine. These rapid changes can come on us like a tsunami, but some can be predicted, seen on the horizon as an impending storm. Often we see a storm coming and we are left with the choice to prepare for it or run for protection. Leading with your strength allows you the opportunity to stand tall and take appropriate measures. Whether it is personal or organizational change blowing your way, be the courageous leader in the midst of the storm. Prepare your heart now to accept and deal with the winds of change.

"So be strong and courageous! Do not be afraid and do not panic before them. For the Lord your God will personally go ahead of you. He will neither fail you nor abandon you."

Deuteronomy 31:6 NLT

Leadership

Applied Project/Program Management

"Winds of Change"

As project/program leaders we are familiar with the criticality of change management. We must have that comprehensive knowledge to create or leverage a change system as we monitor our project's progress. As changes are approved, we will incorporate those changes into the appropriate management plans. In the PMBOK® (*Project Management Body of Knowledge*), the theory and process wrapped around integrated change control is outlined. From project concept through closure, integrated change control can and does occur. Our responsibility as project leaders is to influence requested change as one of the critical roles we play. A key component is to make sure our stakeholders are clear and that we communicate our change control expectations. Also, we need to make a determination if changes have occurred or if they need to occur.

Certainly, we review and approve any requests for change and adjust baselines as appropriate. As approved changes occur, our team implements both corrective and/or applies preventative actions. They make certain we communicate the status of changes implemented to our stakeholders and the impact they have on the project. That's the "science" side of our responsibility to the change process. Let's take a moment for the "art" side of the change process.

Friends, simply put: "Projects change." They just do, and this is the very nature of projects. How we handle change within our teams and with our clients is what makes all the difference. We can embrace the realities of change in a way that is honorable, which means leveraging your experience toward a positive result. Make this the norm. Yes, often change *is* hard, even frustrating at times. It can even be unfair, but keeping your attitude in check can funnel positive energy to your team(s) and your customers, even in the spirit of negotiation. Work through the differences, communicate truthfully and move on. I often test myself to make sure that I am not becoming high maintenance; shoving change aside, the "oh woe is me" type. You know the type, much like the team member who makes us cringe when they call.

Let's all focus on keeping the "art" and "science" side of change management in perspective.

The Perfect Storm

Leadership

"Example is not the main thing in influencing others. It is the only thing."

— *Albert Schweitzer*

As a leader, do those around you see you as the calm in the storm? I often ponder this. We know that things don't always go as planned. When things get chaotic, people need to see us as reassuring and in control. Are you the one they can depend on to help them weather the storm rather than be the storm? This is not easy but required for maintaining the functionality and progress of our teams.

"A generous man will prosper; he who refreshes others will himself be refreshed."

Proverbs 11:25 NIV

Leadership

Applied Project/Program Leadership

"The Perfect Storm"

We all manage projects/programs, whether at home or at work, and we know the pressures which can produce the perfect storm. Often, when managing to our schedule, something will change to impact the timeliness of a pending deliverable, and the storm clouds start to form. We find ourselves scurrying for a solution and customers breathing down our backs. As this happens, keep this thought in the forefront of your mind: "They go as we go." Meaning our leadership demeanor in the face of challenge and change will influence how our team will respond to this situation and others to follow. Will we "act" or "react", calm or crazy?

Friends, it comes down to a choice. When tossed into a challenge or change, consider choosing calm and consider leveraging these guidelines. First, and the toughest to swallow, is, "it's on you." We have chosen to lead so we must own the situation. No pointing fingers, no casting blame, we own it, plain and simple, so let's keep our emotions in check. Next, take time to process what has occurred and don't make a decision based on emotion or immediate circumstance. Take some time to make sure you have the facts reconciled in your mind's eye. Maybe write them down in case chronology is needed. We may need to ask some clarifying questions from others. Seek them out and calmly work through clarification without casting blame or disappointment. Consider an initial solution but don't commit immediately unless it is an emergency. You may choose to gather your leaders together and work through the situation based on the *facts*. Remember to leave the emotion in your back pocket. Iterate what has changed, then pitch your solution to the team as a starting point, but be open to their feedback. Modify the solution as needed with both a primary and secondary solution. When everyone is settled on the approach, bring senior leadership into the mix with the issue, the primary, and secondary solutions. Get your senior leaders buy-in and discuss a strategy to communicate to the customer with both the issue and the possible solutions. Then talk to your customer. Finally, set up a formal meeting to determined lessons learned so this situation doesn't occur a second time. There may be some variation to this approach but the point remains that when the storm hits, "They go, as we go." By approaching this with a sense of urgency and a calm disposition, we can create a working environment of trust and respect in the face of challenge and change.

When all is Said and Done... You Make the Call

Leadership

"It's more important as a manager to be respected than to be popular."

— *Ken Blanchard & Don Shula*

Leadership is not a popularity contest. I have said this a "jillion" times when coaching and mentoring leaders. If you think that the leadership gig is about popularity, then you need to be prepared because you'll be disappointed.

On a daily basis we make dozens of decisions, and we must get used to the fact that we can never please everyone.

Unfortunately, sometimes the best decisions are ones that may let the most people down, but you need to make them just the same.

Resist making decisions based on the popularity of the outcome. Rather, collect the facts from those you trust, leverage your experience, and knowledge, and then *YOU* make the call.

"Give me an understanding heart so that I can govern your people well and know the difference between right and wrong. For who by himself is able to govern this great people of yours?"

1 Kings 3:9 NLT

Leadership

Applied Project/Program Management

"When All is Said and Done... You Make the Call"

I once had a unique opportunity to chat about leadership philosophies with a pilot from United Airlines. This was especially riveting as he explained his company's leadership philosophy. He said that each decision is based on the impact of each "soul" on board the aircraft. As my curiosity peaked, I asked him specifically about their tactics for making such tough calls. I was amazed at his quick and confident response.

He said, "Steve, it really isn't that complicated and often not popular. We are trained to discuss those big decisions with the crew in the cockpit. We expect them to provide their opinions based on the facts they have at hand. Then, the captain makes the call.

- I listen intently and have trust in their ability, insight and experience.
- I check to see what the 'instruments' reveal.
- I check in with air traffic control in the tower for their take on the situation, etc.
- I factor in what the instruments, my crew, the tower and what my own training and experience are telling me.
- Then, I make the call and everyone honors it."

As project/program leaders, we can learn from this pilot's example as we make the tougher decisions and judgment calls.

"None of us is as smart as all of us" — a famous quote by best-selling Author, Ken Blanchard. When we face big decisions that may make or break our projects or could influence/impact those we lead, bring your leaders and/or trusted team members together to gather their input. Then *you* make the call.

People in most cases don't have the innate need to have their own way, they do, however, desire to have their opinions listened to and factored into the decision. This practice will create and facilitate the development of trust on your team and throughout your organization.

Keep Your Vision Clear

Leadership

"Vision is knowing who are you, where you're going and what will guide your journey."

— Ken Blanchard and Jesse Stoner

Let me confess that this one has been difficult for me, as we are all working at such a fast pace. Sometimes I want to get ahead of myself so I struggle with this, and it is so critical.

Leadership giant Ken Blanchard says: "Vision is a lot more than a plaque on the wall — real vision is lived not framed." Steven Covey writes: "Start with the end in mind." This concept has actually been around so long that we can even read it in the Bible: "Where there is no vision, the people perish." This means that people need to know where they are going. No matter how good we plan, if we don't fit into the overall vision, we are not really fulfilling all the areas of our job. Often when I speak to groups on this topic I hear comments that this is the responsibility of the board of directors or the vice presidents, but it isn't their job, certainly not at the project or program level. This is not true and is short-sided thinking. We must rally our teams with a target that means something to everyone involved over the long haul and over communicate it.

Will you lead a team that is simply building a structure that won't fall down before the contract ends, or do they have a vision of serving the residents who will use that building for the next hundred years?

"My son, preserve sound judgment and discernment, do not let them out of your sight."

Proverbs 3:21 NIV

Leadership

Applied Project/Program Management

"Keep Your Vision Clear"

When we put on our many project/program manager hats, we might think we spend the majority of our time developing the plans for our projects, and most often we do. We know the importance of planning. In the grand scheme of things planning is simple. Sure it takes a while to learn and a lifetime to master, but when compared to vision, it is really child's play. Think about it in terms of the project, team and/or organization you lead. When the plan changes for whatever reason, if people don't understand the new direction they are suppose to be headed in, if they don't have a good road map, what happens? People get irritable and restless and often unkind. Team members can get "glitchy" over time because they don't know where they are going. They may be working hard and may find their own direction within their smaller circles of influence. Maybe they will navigate through the shorter deliverables on their own, but this will only last for a while. As a team, they will become scattered all over the map. In short order, the majority of team members will stop taking the project and even the organization seriously; you and your leadership will start to wane.

I contend that too many of us substitute planning, even great planning, for vision. We're so wrapped up in planning the trip that we forget to find out what the vacation is supposed to be about. We must help our teams understand where they fit into the bigger picture. They must understand that what they do is helping the stakeholders, project, and the overall organization. There are consequences for lack of vision. People will begin to believe that the organization and project lacks vision and even take their eyes off the goal. They'll begin to look at other projects and decide they would rather be with people who really know where they are going and why. Work motivations and aspirations begin to fall away and team members will detach from the project and the organization.

As project/program leaders, we must take the necessary steps to develop and maintain a clear and well-communicated vision.

It's a Pressure Cooker

Leadership

"Only by contending with challenges that seem to be beyond your strength to handle at the moment can you grow more surely toward the stars."

— Brian Tracy

Hang in there! The pressures we face in leadership can cause discouragement and this can sometimes make you feel like you just want to surrender and pack it in.

Nobody said it was going to be easy. By developing your leadership skill set anything is possible.

Make the investment in yourself and be confident. The sky is truly the limit — enable your competence to become excellent at what you do.

"But as for you, be strong and do not give up, for your work will be rewarded."

2 Chronicles 15:7 NIV

Leadership

Applied Project/Program Management

"It's a Pressure Cooker"

We have all been there, or maybe you are there right now. Sometimes the pressure of your project/program can crush your spirit. Often the problems seem overwhelming; while at other times it may be an issue that is just an annoyance. Either way, we must dig in and work toward a solution.

Even the more challenging problems need a strategy to get to the root cause. Always look at the facts and don't get caught up in the emotion. This isn't easy to do when you have project pressures breathing down your neck.

Depending on the size and complexity of the problem(s) you are facing, consider a meeting with your leadership or a simple review in a status meeting. Plan and assign actions to deal with the core of the problem. Then execute your plan and take action steps to resolve it.

I know it isn't always as simple as I have explained it here, but if we understand the importance of leading through problem resolution by *acting* and not *reacting* we can:

- Minimize the project/program pressure;
- Resolve the problem;
- Receive a vote of confidence from the team; and
- Bring about a solution.

This is a good formula for problem resolution that will minimize project pressure!

Enthusiastically Yours

Leadership

"Catch on fire with enthusiasm and people will come from miles to watch you burn."

— John Wesley

Not long ago I prepared and delivered a critical program update to my leadership and staff team. The meeting was long and intense, and I was scheduled to present toward the end of the meeting. When it was finally my turn, the energy level in the room was at an all-time low. As I looked around, everyone in the room looked like cadavers. In that moment I had to make a choice. Should I modify my presentation to be shorter and take the "let's just get it done" road, or rise to the challenge and jump-start this room out of its coma? An easy choice, so I went for it. I had a conservative start to warm up the room, yet the further I got into the presentation the more animated I became. I stood up at one point to direct attention to a slide, this caught the room completely by surprise and I quickly noticed more anticipation and attention from everyone watching. The energy turned into synergy, and my presentation turned into an enthusiastic team discussion. **Gosh, that was fun!**

I bet we all enjoy getting the people around us charged up to rally around our area of interest. However, the real rush is the transference of the good stuff fostering momentum to bring people to the edge of their seat with dialogue flowing across the table and around the room. Moreover, it's the value and what the attendees take away, remember, and work on long after the meeting is adjourned.

Enthusiastically Yours,

Steve

Leadership

Applied Project/Program Management

"Enthusiastically Yours"

Are you believable? Often times in our project leadership we have circumstances when we must deliver information to encourage and motivate our project teams. It could be delivering a program vision, charging up the troops to meet a tough deadline, or maybe something as simple as a project status report. I have seen outstanding leaders energize a team or an audience with almost no preparation. Oh, what a gift! If you are like me, it's all about knowing your audience and being prepared... to being over prepared. Dodge the naysayers that encourage you to "wing it" or tell you to "go with your gut" and forget a formal preparation when delivering an important message to your team or leadership. The bottom line is that our teams and leaders deserve the best we can give. Here are four quick and simple guidelines that have helped me over the years.

- Know your audience! If it is a group of senior leaders, don't go into the weeds; rather, give them the high-level stuff. If it is a team presentation, dig in and get into the details.

- Search for your audience's hot button to coincide with your presentation and prepare an outline. A reference document will assist you in hitting those hot buttons spot on to drive the energy and discussion level up a notch or two.

- Don't just give them the "what to do". Make sure you spend some of your time on the "whys" *and* how it will impact them and the value it will bring to the project/program and/or the client.

- Give them all of your energy and enthusiasm. But don't fake it, as those attending will see right through you.

Finally, don't *only* deliver the good news, nothing is ever perfect and every project/program has issues. They will expect to hear both the positive as well as the challenges they face.

Build a "Leadership Circle"

Leadership

"Interdependent people combine their own efforts with the efforts of others to achieve their greatest success."

— Stephen Covey

Wouldn't it be something to know the best response for our most difficult leadership decisions? Responding to the toughest issues not only with compassion but also with greater certainty will maximize our leadership ability. It could be a number of things like a serious situation with a teammate or a customer seeking our wisdom for the challenges they face, etc.

Build a "leadership circle" around yourself and bring great minds together. This should be a small group of leaders you can trust and turn to in any situation. Individuals you can always count on when the chips are down. These should be people who will not judge you but tell you the truth, not just what you *want* to hear. Gradually build your circle with caution and care. Discuss openly the importance of confidentiality and accountability with one another. This "leadership circle" will become an extension of how you lead.

"Plans go wrong for lack of advice; many advisers bring success."

Proverbs 15:22

Leadership

Applied Project/Program Management

"Build a Leadership Circle"

I am not sure about you, but for me there are times when I feel like I am leading without a compass. I know I have a destination, a desired end result, but there are dozens of decisions along the way. The enumerable choices I can make are critical, and they will impact people. The bottom line is sometimes we are just too close to the issue(s) to make the best call. But having a second, maybe even a third opinion, makes good leadership sense.

I believe that every project/program manager should have a core team of leaders they can utilize for advice. This team does not have to be members of your project/program; in fact, they shouldn't be.

Your team of leaders should consist of two to three trustworthy, credible and available leaders you can turn to for project/program advice, direction, or to talk you through critical decisions both long and short-term. Conversely, they will be able to get the same counsel from you. This team will be vital to your success and growth as a leader, so choose these individuals wisely. Your instincts will guide you as to who to choose, and in my experience they will be excited and anxious to participate. Then, set up formal meetings and meet as often as this team feels appropriate. I have found every two weeks works well. Determine the essence of the meetings — yes, build an agenda — so the meeting is valuable for all parties.

Then ride the wave with an honest, open interchange with a group of people who share mutual respect for one another. This inner circle of leaders will prove to be one of the best leadership decisions you will ever make.

Turn Your Back to the Crowd

Leadership

"A leader, once convinced that a particular course of action is the right one, must be undaunted when the going gets tough."

— Ronald Reagan

I recently had the privilege of speaking with Jeff Tyzik, the Principal Pops Conductor of the Rochester, NY Philharmonic Orchestra. What a brilliant, talented man, who I found to have great wisdom on leadership. I asked several questions and was amazed at his answers. As I probed deeper, Jeff gave me a ton of insight, but there was one leadership example he shared with me that I will never forget. He mentioned that his leadership role is unique both literally and figuratively. To conduct his orchestra, he must turn his back to the crowd and pay attention to his musicians — his team. As he makes leadership decisions and choices, some may be unpopular, influencing those he cares about and the impact for some can feel much like he is turning his back on them.

Someone will inevitably get caught in the wake of a decision, which is often an unfortunate circumstance, but it is the nature of our role as leaders.

Over the years, many leaders have asked me what the best advice I can give them is, and I always answer: "If you are in this leadership role for the popularity, you need to find another gig."

"I've commanded you to be strong and brave. Don't ever be afraid or discouraged! I am the LORD your God, and I will be there to help you wherever you go."

Joshua 1:9 CEV

Leadership

Applied Project/Program Management

"Turn Your Back on the Crowd"

Not long ago, I made a program decision that was very unpopular. One team member expressed strong verbal discontent, and it influenced others. Yet, every leadership bone in my body knew I had made the right call. This decision was not easy, and I didn't take it lightly. It wasn't made in a vacuum or on a whim. I did my homework. Here is how I came to my decision.

- I investigated what other programs had done and were doing;
- I spoke to several experts who had completed initiatives much like the one I was planning;
- I talked through the concept with several trusted leaders;
- I revisited the mission of the program;
- I looked at the program objectives to make sure I was working to meet those objectives and to ensure this initiative was in alignment;
- I pored through past performance, trends and historical information;
- I looked at the potential resources available; and
- I prayed fervently for wisdom.

Not every decision needs this kind of research and attention, but the big ones that influence change and create challenges need this level of analysis and discretion. When we have done our due diligence and make the tough call, we need to **stand by our decision!** My decision turned out to be the correct one for the program, but some of my decisions have not. In this particular case one individual felt like maybe I had turned my back on them. Not popular but correct just the same.

Friendly advice: If a decision goes south, be careful not to hide behind those you sought information and then cast a shadow of blame their way. We need to own it, learn from it, recalibrate, and then be ready to make the next tough call that comes our way.

Mucus Trooper

Leadership

(MYOO.kus troo.pur) *n.* An employee with a cold or the flu who insists on showing up for work. — mucus troop *v.*

www.wordspy.com/words/mucustrooper.asp

Nice title, huh? Sometimes when making a point we need some comic relief. There are real issues in the workplace when managing people and dealing with delicate issues. However, you can make this fun just the same.

I recently conducted a workshop for a group of leaders using the words and definitions (on the next page) to present "How to Maintain a Healthy Work Environment." These are comical and in some cases a bit exaggerated. Yet, you will find them to be quite true. All credit goes to Paul McFedries of www.wordspy.com. Have some fun and check out this website.

"There is a time to cry and a time to laugh. There is a time to be sad and a time to dance."

Ecclesiastes 3:4 NCV

Leadership

Applied Project/Program Management

"Mucus Trooper"

Here are some tools you can use to help develop a healthy work environment... enjoy! (Visit: www.wordspy.com for more.)

Presenteeism:

http://www.wordspy.com/words/presenteeism.asp

n. The feeling that one must show up for work even if one is too sick, stressed, or distracted to be productive; the feeling that one needs to work extra hours even if one has no extra work to do. — **presentee** *n.*

Rat-race equilibrium:

www.wordspy.com/words/rat-raceequilibrium.asp

n. A workplace balance in which an employee's willingness to work long hours for possible promotion is equal to an employer's belief that working long hours merits promotion.

Vacation deprivation:

www.wordspy.com/words/vacationdeprivation.asp

n. Foregoing vacation days because of busyness at work. — **vacation deprived** *adj.*

Sleep Camel:

www.wordspy.com/words/sleepcamel.asp

n. A person who gets little sleep during the week, and then attempts to make up for it by sleeping in and napping on the weekend.

Corporate anorexia:

www.wordspy.com/words/corporateanorexia.asp

n. A business disorder marked by an extreme fear of becoming inefficient which leads to excessive cost-cutting to the point of serious loss of business and sometimes bankruptcy.

Cheer for the Underdog

Leadership

"It is literally true that you can succeed best and quickest by helping others to succeed."

— Napoleon Hill, 1883-1970

One of my top five sports movies of all time is *Rudy*. You may know the story of this inspirational football practice player from Notre Dame who pushed himself to his physical limits as he diligently and passionately pursued his dream to play in a Notre Dame football game.

It has always been my nature to cheer for the underdog. At sporting events and even during a good movie I find myself hoping the underdog wins the game or gets the prize. For my project team, it's the same thing. When there is someone like "Rudy", who is working hard to learn in a stretch position and is coachable, I make it my business to go out of my way to coach, mentor and assist that individual. When a teammate is taking on a new challenge, we need to take that extra step to set them up for success. It will be a victory for your teammate, and over the long haul you will get way more than you bargained for.

"As iron sharpens iron, so people can improve each other."

Proverbs 27:17 (NCV)

Leadership

Applied Program/Project Leadership

"Cheer for the Underdog"

Over a decade ago I started working in a new company. In my first PM engagement I was tossed into a huge and troubled project with restless clients. I was sent to St. Louis, MO with almost no knowledge of the situation. This was my first engagement, and I wanted give a great first impression to my new employer, and yes, I was the underdog. Frankly, I was a bit nervous. When I got off the plane at the St. Louis Airport, I was met by a fellow employee who liked to be called "Harv". I was dressed in a suit and Harv, a seemingly jolly fellow, had on a big ol' cowboy hat on with jeans and cowboy boots. I thought, "What did I get myself into?" He welcomed me in kind, I got the rental car and I followed him to the hotel. After we got to the hotel and checked in, we met a short time later. To my surprise Harv dug in! He spent the next several hours getting me up to speed and outlining specific client needs from top to bottom. Yet, what I appreciated most were his words that I have never forgotten. He said, "Steve, we are together on this, and there is no way we will fail with this client." We worked together with this client for six months, and things couldn't have gone better... thanks to Harv!

The *Project Management Body of Knowledge* (PMBOK®) tells us that our project budget should include training dollars to train our people to have the proper skill set for the project/program. I think we need to do more, and so did Harv. In our projects we may find a functional leader or project coordinator that has good intentions but may lack experience. Maybe this role is the next step in their career journey. It will be the experience they gain in the role that could bring them to the next level of their career, or it could drive them down.

So "Harv" them! I believe we need to step up and take the opportunity to help shape a future leader by offering our experience and expertise. Offer to coach or mentor them and be sure to make your offer formal. This will foster the best opportunity for success for the individual and your project/ program. It will create a dynamic accountability partnership with your project success as the primary goal.

Knowledge Yields Respect
Leadership

"Practice Golden-Rule 1 of Management in everything you do. Manage others the way you would like to be managed."

— *Brian Tracy*

As leaders, how we treat others must always be in the forefront of our mind. Whatever team we are responsible for leading, gaining respect from that team is a privilege, and one we must earn. Gaining the respect of those we lead is hard, humbling and impossible to fake.

One way is to challenge ourselves daily to remain vulnerable and plan our actions based on what is right for those in our charge.

Another biggie is to keep our skills and knowledge razor sharp around the leadership trends and discipline.

At the end of the day it's all about what we can do to serve our team!

"In this world the kings and great men order their people around, and yet they are called 'friends of the people.' But among you, those who are the greatest should take the lowest rank, and the leader should be like a servant."

Luke 22:25-26 NLT

Leadership

Applied Project/Program Leadership

"Knowledge Yields Respect"

The Project Human Resource Management knowledge area, PMI® talks about the "powers of a project manager". These "powers" are sometimes referred to as ways to get cooperation from your stakeholders; which by the way includes your team members. One "power of the project manager" is expert, meaning you are seen by most on the project to be the project management expert. Project managers enhance their credibility and respect from knowing and understanding our complex discipline. This also contributes to gaining professional respect in terms of having an in-depth knowledge of both the tactical and strategic areas of project methodology. We owe it to ourselves to stay current with trends in all the process and knowledge areas of project management so we can serve in our greatest capacity. I encourage you to look for ways to enhance and maintain your PM expertise.

One approach is to acquire a PMI® credential in project management: "PMI® credentials establish your dedication to and proficiency in project management," as stated by PMI®. Here are a couple of credentials that I would recommend:

The Certified Associate in Project Management, (CAPM®) Project Management Professional (PMP), Program Management Professional (PgMP®).

PMI® offers several other professional credentials to assist you in maintaining your level of professional credibility, expertise and gaining professional respect. If you have not taken the step to getting a credential, I would encourage you to do so. You won't regret it! (www.pmi.org).

Make Your Meetings Memorable

Leadership

"Having a simple, clearly defined goal can capture the imagination and inspire passion. It can cut through the fog like a beacon in the night."

— *Unknown*

The concept of preparing well thought-out meetings may sound overly simplistic. This is one area that is very much abused. When this happens, it is just bad news and quite expensive. We all have lots of meetings, but do we try to make each one mean something? Typically, people will show up on time, prepared, and even in some cases you may have an attendee or two energized. But will everyone show up ready to contribute? Think about it, when we anticipate attending a meeting knowing we will be bored to tears, we will look for every excuse to miss the meeting. Also, with time so tight in our workday, nobody wants to give away even an hour of useless time at a useless meeting with no real or relevant outcomes. What about falling into a trap and finding yourself meeting for meeting's sake?

It is easy to get into a rut on a long-term project, or if you are with a team for an extended period of time. Exercise your creativity. Each month take a moment to reassess those recurring meetings to determine their effectiveness and relevance. Better yet, meet with a confidant and ask them if they are getting what you hoped from your meetings that they attend. You might be surprised at their response.

"Walk in wisdom toward outsiders, making the best use of the time. Let your speech always be gracious, seasoned with salt, so that you may know how you ought to answer each person."

Colossians 4:5-6 ESV

Leadership

Applied Project/Program Management

"Make Your Meetings Memorable"

It is important how we facilitate meetings and something we must not take lightly. Poor meeting facilitation can be a disaster for maintaining the integrity of an effective meeting, and in the long run it reflects on the credibility of our leadership. I know every meeting can't be a grand slam, but we should give it our best effort. Here are some steps I have practiced over the years that you may find helpful:

- Always remember to have an agenda. Actually, I think anyone can "build" an agenda, but we really should "architect" the agenda in a way that makes the meeting engaging.
- Determine a meeting objective. Ask yourself: "What is it we want to accomplish in the meeting?"
- Consider a five-minute icebreaker, but not for every meeting.
- Determine what will be the desired outcome of each agenda item. Meaning, for most topics what you want to "get" from the discussion, an outcome or output from those attending.

Item #	Time	Agenda topic	Desired Outcome	Owner

- Make sure you invite the right people. Having the wrong people can create personal agendas and distractions. Furthermore, make it relevant to all attending. When meetings are not relevant to what the attendees are working on, people will not want to come, and they will not attend.
- Have fun but facilitate with diligence and zeal. Use your meetings to encourage and engage in healthy conflict, making sure you have set team conflict expectations to keep healthy debates in check.
- Stick to your agenda, whenever people go off in the weeds, time is wasted and all the others will disengage.
- With five minutes remaining in your meeting, remember to review all the decisions and actions.
- *ALWAYS* start and end on time! Honoring attendee's time shows you respect them. They will gain confidence and trust in your ability to facilitate meetings within the time parameters communicated.

MOST OF ALL... Remember, the meeting is not for you, it is for them.

Influence and Direction

Leadership

"Leadership rests not only upon ability, not only upon capacity; having the capacity to lead is not enough. The leader must be willing to use it. His leadership is then based on truth and character. There must be truth in the purpose and will power in the character."

— Vince Lombardi

Merriam-Webster defines *"follower"* to be or act in accordance with <*follow* directions>: to accept as authority.

Believe it or not, people on your team(s) crave direction and discipline. The truth is most people are content to be followers. It is hard to get them to admit it, but if you have earned respect from your teams, you will see your direction, mentoring and leadership shape what they do, who they are, and even how they behave. Our leadership is only successful when those on our team(s) are willing to participate in the direction we give them. This is our test of trust, respect, knowledge and ability.

We must not take our leadership lightly or take it for granted. Consider your leadership influence as a privilege.

"Care for the flock that God has entrusted to you. Watch over it willingly, not grudgingly—not for what you will get out of it, but because you are eager to serve God. Don't lord it over the people assigned to your care, but lead them by your own good example. And when the Great Shepherd appears, you will receive a crown of never-ending glory and honor."

1 Peter 5:2-4 NLT

Leadership

Applied Project and Program Management

"Influence and Direction"

I was asked to lead a new project, and unfortunately planning started out quite slow. This was not necessarily a bad thing, it was just a bit slower than I am typically used to. Part of the issue was wrapped around the uniqueness of the project being a complimentary project to another already going on for a number of months. With shifts in process, funding, sponsors, resources and other areas, all decisions that needed to be made were somewhat unusual to keep the project moving, especially under these weird circumstances. We had a smaller team, but the constant shift in the project was somewhat trying on all of us. From the get-go and in many conversations wrapped around project direction and decisions, I have been challenged by team members, who bring excellent wisdom to the table. I LOVE THAT!

As project managers in a well-managed project, we influence and have the ultimate decision-making and final authority. Depending on how we handle this responsibility could ultimately impact our leadership in the near AND long term.

The first week of the project I spoke to my team members regarding expectations, project decisions, direction and communications. I am a believer that we are each blessed with a talent(s). My expectation is that each maximizes and shares their gift, skill, and knowledge in what they do. This ultimately, and in fact, will influence our teams greatly toward success and/or failure of the project. Also, and equally important, an expectation of influence by sharing opinions openly and honestly in regards to the situation but respectfully to me and other teammates.

Setting expectations, reminding our teams of their talents, and the influence and the impact of those talents, along with consideration of their opinions will grow our leadership and build individual confidence. Most importantly, it will act as a building block toward a trusting team environment.

Don't Cower

Leadership

"Servant-leadership encourages collaboration, trust, foresight, listening, and the ethical use of power and empowerment"

— Letze Oostinga, MA MGM

Don't cower, stand straight to face the challenges of each day, be truthful, ethical and upstanding. Confront and always speak the truth with kindness and compassion.

I witnessed a leader's situation a few years back that was somewhat disturbing. Here is the short story version:

An organization lost their two top leaders within a six-month period. An individual was asked to stand in on a part-time basis to lead their small leadership team for an interim period. He was asked to manage, monitor, and measure the progress of the small leadership team over the course of several months and report their progress back to a governing body/group. This small yet very capable team of leaders typically performed well, however, they were used to being on their own with little formality and little to no support or structure. Often this led to a lack of efficiency and zero accountability.

As the new leader began to suggest change to increase efficiency and accountability, most in the group caught on quickly and enjoyed the growth of their teams with increased success measures, while others stumbled a bit, much like many groups do when adjusting to new leadership. Performance began to increase mainly by creating and accomplishing goals, and for many the challenge of change turned into success and growth.

As I mentioned, most of the team caught on, but not everyone. The few leaders that did not catch on couldn't or simply chose not to participate. They started to stage a mini-coup. A few of these leaders became "poison pills", and they began pulling others, along with the new leader, down with them. Because the change was rapid, people sadly started to point fingers and turned the success and growth into negative circumstances. They even began having private meetings which simply inflamed the situation.

From time to time this situation can be found in unstable organizations, but it can be rectified. In this case, the leader did the right thing by setting up numerous meetings to speak to those fueling the conflict. Unfortunately, they made excuses to not attend the meetings to resolve the conflict, so the meetings never happened. When the leader escalated the issue to the governing body/group, the situation was looked upon as a "personality flaw" of the new leader, and he was let go instead of governing body confronting the real issue. The senior leadership cowered, and the real problem was both left unsolved, thus the problem was transferred to the next leader. Bad Leadership 101. The governing body/group brought in a new leader to "facilitate change", yet they never confronted the "poison pills" barriers to much-needed change. Needless to say, within one year another leader moved on and sadly the organization is still in turmoil.

Teams need leaders to serve team members, and they need a leader to build into them and support them, especially if they are right in making hard decisions. Teams also need leaders who are willing to confront those that are *not* on board to remedy a dysfunctional team/bad team scenario, and senior leaders *must* believe in it, support it, and deal with it. Experience tells us most times that this is very difficult. However, if we cower, ignore or try to smooth over the situation, the problem always escalates, and this does not serve the team or the organization well. Always keep in mind that avoidance never makes a problem go away, avoiding it will always make the problem bigger. So, I end this short story as I started: Stand straight in the face of adversity, be truthful, and upstanding. Confront and speak with kindness and compassion... and always speak the truth.

"Instead, speaking the truth in love, we will in all things grow up into him who is the Head, that is, Christ."

Ephesians 4:15 (NIV)

Leadership
Applied Project/Program Leadership
"Don't Cower"

One day at the grocery store I ran into a friend who owns a small business and has several employees. He was frustrated because he is continually losing employees. He is a good person and a good friend, but he can never seem to put his finger on why people come and go from his business so quickly. As he shared his plight he said: "I don't get why people don't understand that when I say jump, they should just ask how high?" We didn't chat any further that day, but he must have seen the surprised look on my face to hear him make such a comment. This time he had it wrong. Don't cower doesn't mean "boss people around". In our last leadership example, senior leadership ignored a "poison pill" problem then failed to support the leader's action to do what was right and confront the issue. In this example, our small-business owner is taking the aggressive "I am always right" attitude.

Projects/programs offer a unique opportunity to flex our leadership muscle. Teams depend on us to make decisions in the heat of the project and often our decisions are unpopular but necessary just the same. Some might consider a dictatorial/autocratic approach and others may not. Managing a project is dependent on how we lead the people on our teams. In fact, we must determine the most appropriate leadership style for the current need of the project depending where we are in the project. PMI® suggests choices like: directing, facilitating, coaching, supporting, autocratic, consultative, and consensus leadership styles. Many studies offer suggestions as to which style is most appropriate depending on where we are in the project. As a general rule, project managers typically provide more direction in the front end of a project. As we move through execution, we find ourselves involved more with supporting, coaching or facilitating our teams.

I would like to suggest this one leadership theory as we all continue to work hard as leaders of our projects/programs. Consider "servant leadership" as your primary approach. In essence, servant leadership is our opportunity to be a leader that serves our team. I encourage you to create an environment whereupon our team's or individual's highest priority needs are being served. There are dozens of articles out there today, but I love what Letze Oostinga, MA MGM, says in the article: *Leading by Serving First Explanation of Servant-Leadership of Robert K. Greenleaf:* "Servant-leadership encourages collaboration, trust, foresight, listening, and the ethical use of power and empowerment." Examples of servant-leader traits include: listening, empathy, awareness, foresight, stewardship, commitment to growth of people and building community.

I'll bet most of us practice or aspire to lead by incorporating these servant-leadership traits. Take a moment in your own personal and professional growth to assess where you are, your style of leadership, and consider the steps you need to take to grow as a servant leader.

Source:
http://www.12manage.com/methods_greenleaf_servant_leadership.html

Chapter 2

Humility

Confidence vs. Arrogance...It's a Fine Line
Humility

"If what you're seeking is lasting relationships, long-term success and quality of life in all areas then you will be better served to forego the pompous acts of the arrogant for the humility and quiet confidence displayed by true leaders."

— Unknown

I was a huge fan of the TV series *The West Wing*, and I am sad to this day that the series ended after seven seasons. It was intriguing to see such high respect for the office and position of the president portrayed in every episode. In one specific episode a new policymaker and speechwriter, Will Bailey, played by Joshua Malina, was meeting the president for the first time. In this scene Will was outrageously nervous and intimidated in his first opportunity to discuss an issue with President Bartlet, played by Martin Sheen. In this interchange, President Bartlet and his senior advisors in the Oval Office were testing Will to see if he would express his opinion to someone in power.

As we grow more mature in our career, we have moments when we are asked for our opinions and/or feedback by those serving in higher-level positions that know much less about the PM discipline and area of specialty. Rise to the occasion and opportunity with courage, conviction, confidence, and most of all passion. One small caution, in the heat of moment, don't mistake confidence for arrogance.

Oh by the way, "Will" was able to successfully deliver his opinion to the President and his senior advisors with passion, poise and confidence. He also earned a few notches on their respect meter.

"For I can do everything through Christ, who gives me strength."
Philippians 4:13 NLT

Humility

Applied Project/Program Management

"Confidence vs. Arrogance...It's a Fine Line"

Delivering a message to multiple audiences of project stakeholders takes on its own challenges. Giving status updates to a project team and updates to senior leadership is a completely different endgame. To our immediate project team, dig into the details, but senior management, not so much detail.

In a recent program role, I was asked to report a monthly program status to a vice president and his leadership team. We must learn quickly the balance of reporting to an audience of senior leaders. Key things to consider: Get a clear objective as to what your *audience* wants to hear. You need to hit *their* mark of expectation.

- Anticipate questions they might ask and be prepared to provide answers.
- Prepare intently and consider: Where you have been, where you are now, and where you are going?
- Rehearse out loud what you want to say prior to presenting. Believe it or not, key points will come back to you.
- Be passionate and confident. You may only have ten minutes to knock them out of their chairs.
- Provide less detail, fewer bullet points but more substance. Stay at the milestone level, no deeper.
- Present no more than three slides. Use short phrases or simple diagrams on your slides. Consider the "Seven Rule". No more than seven bullets and no more than seven words for each bullet.
- Give key successes in terms of tangible numbers THEY would want to hear. Keep it high-level, not too detailed.
- Resist making it entirely about successes. Every project faces some issues. Present the top issue, the plan to resolve it, and the status of the plan.
- Make sure you give them time to ask questions.
- Finally, when you are finished, thank them for the opportunity to present.

The Ego Meter

Humility

"The key to successful leadership is influence, not authority."
— *Ken Blanchard*

I love what Ken Blanchard says, and he couldn't be more right. We need to keep an eye on our ego meter. We are all human, and from time to time we become vulnerable and our alter ego will raise its ugly head. Quickly, our influence turns to authority and we become a less effective, disrespected leader.

"Pride comes before destruction and an arrogant spirit before a fall."

Proverbs 16:18 (HCSB)

Humility

Applied Project/Program Leadership

"The Ego Meter"

As project managers, I bet we have all seen leaders and managers over the years that are full of themselves. They are so impressed with themselves that they lose the respect of their team and other leaders in the organization. Sadly, in some cases they actually seem to like it.

Our responsibility is much less about people doing what we order and much more about serving our greater team. Taking that attitude will create a team dynamic where the project/program manager will have earned the respect of each team member. As leaders, let's be sure to check our ego at the door.

Proud Not Prideful

Humility

"It was pride that changed angels into devils; it is humility that makes men as angels."

— *Saint Augustine*

I just don't see anything wrong with being proud of work well done, if (a BIG "if") we are not prideful.

It is one thing to work hard and accomplish great things. It is entirely another to puff yourself up with pride and boastful disregard.

Pride is the enemy of credibility.

"For those who exalt themselves will be humbled, and those who humble themselves will be exalted."

Luke 18:14 NLT

Humility

Applied Project/Program Leadership

"Proud Not Prideful"

Can you remember a time when you worked for a leader that took all the credit for project/program successes when in reality dozens of people created the success?

Project and program managers need to work diligently to remind those we have the privilege to work with how much they contribute, how much we appreciate them, and all their good work. This isn't something we do as an extra thing; rather, it should be part of our DNA as a leader.

Think in terms of the "mirror and window". When things are going great, look out the window and see the extraordinary work your team is doing. Then, be sure to tell them so. However, when you are faced with more challenging project/program issues and things may not be going so well, we must stop and look in the mirror.

As leaders, we need to own the criticism and accountability that comes with the responsibility of leadership.

Don't Doubt the Benefit

Humility

"To forgive is to set a prisoner free and discover that the prisoner was you."

— Lewis B. Smedes

I think it is safe to say that we have all had those experiences where people are disloyal, or they betray us, or break promises. This is tough stuff, yet it is a big part of what we experience in leadership and also in our everyday lives.

I once heard a very powerful message about forgiveness that I have never forgotten. The first half of the message suggested that holding on to bad feelings about someone — i.e. holding a "grudge" — needs to be avoided at all costs and forgiveness must be extended. I have worked hard to live by these words. The second half of the message was very insightful when the teacher said to not confuse "forgiveness" with "relationship". If a co-worker, friend or family member has been grossly disrespectful, dishonest, or has betrayed you in some capacity, it is our responsibility to forgive them, and I'm good with that. However, in the same vein, based on that forgiveness, we don't have to feel obligated to maintain a relationship with that person. It is a choice, and practicing great restraint not to facilitate a relationship under these adverse circumstances has fared very well and benefitted both my professional and personal relationships.

"Then Peter came to him and asked, 'Lord, how often should I forgive someone who sins against me? Seven times?' 'No, not seven times,' Jesus replied, 'but seventy times seven!'"

Mathew 18:21-22 NLT

Humility

Applied Project/Program Leadership

"Don't Doubt the Benefit"

In building our teams we have a lot to think about and act upon. In most organizations we can observe a great deal of talent diversity. By surrounding ourselves with multiple talents, we can introduce a team environment that will maximize the benefits of those talents.

In many project environments often we are given resources based on their availability. Other times, and not often enough, we can choose our own team members. Certainly we should not want to select team members to be a clone of ourselves. If we did, it would create a team that lacks the benefit of diversity in talent and expertise that is needed for a project. However, in our selection process we must set the bar and our expectations high. But we must keep achievable expectations. It's a tough balance, but here are a few guidelines that have served me well when choosing teams to get the greatest benefit:

- If someone has a long history of questionable ethics, disrespect or dishonesty, be careful. They say, in many cases, "A leopard never changes its spots." Behavior patterns ultimately turn to habits. New behaviors will need to be established... no small task in itself.

- Resist the "I can change them" mentality both for the short and long term. Typically, you can't change someone (unless maybe you are a hypnotherapist). We certainly can "influence" and provide role model behavior, however, they must choose to change, and that is never a guarantee. Maybe a "tough love" conversation would serve the situation, but when it's time to decide if they stay or go, follow your leadership instincts.

- Spend some time with those you are considering and check in with other leaders you respect who have worked with them in the past to get their feedback.

- Choose really smart people who have the qualities, skills and experience you lack.

There are many more, but these are the big ones that have been effective throughout my leadership tenure and yielded exceptional benefits.

The Blessing of Success

Humility

> *"When it comes to life the critical thing is whether you take things for granted or take them with gratitude."*
>
> G. K. Chesterton

My wife and I recently visited my oldest son, Pete, in Los Angeles. During our visit we all chatted about our jobs and the successes we have experienced. As a twenty-seven-year-old, Pete is relatively new in his career and has done things right to start strong and his momentum is growing. In fact, we are rather proud of what he has achieved.

As we chatted, I shared with him this life lesson that I always keep in the forefront of my mind. That is to never, *never,* take for granted the blessing of having a job and a career path. We work *long* and *hard* to develop our career and serve in a job we love. This creates an opportunity that can yield career success.

Be wise and never forget that as long as it takes to achieve success, it can be gone in a moment. Work hard and *never* take it for granted.

"Let all that I am praise the Lord; may I never forget the good things he does for me."

Psalm 103:2 NLT

Humility

Applied Project/Program Management

"The Blessing of Success"

You have all heard it said that "Success breeds success," and we can all agree that it never comes without good old-fashioned hard work. I love what I do, and I try to never take it for granted as a building block of success in my life and my projects. Mostly, I marvel that I have the blessing of a job role that feels like part of my DNA as an individual. Most of all, I love it when a plan comes together, in fact, I bet we all do! It's how we are wired as project/program managers.

That said, as we develop our projects/programs, we are reminded of the critical nature of starting/initiating our project(s) toward a successful outcome. We know getting it right in the front end by being diligent with our start-up can and will alleviate many downturns during monitoring and control toward a successful end result. In fact, great planning in the front end could save you big money and effort in the back end.

Know your stuff and don't be bullied into compromising your initiating activities. Ultimately, we are the ones held accountable for the success of the project.

Here are some things to consider in initiating your project/program:

- Consider getting formal authorization to start your project (Project Charter);
- During initiating, your initial scope can be defined (Scope Statement);
- Financial resources may be identified and committed, and
- Both internal and external stakeholders can be identified (Stakeholder Register, Stakeholder Management Strategy).

This will give you a jumpstart on the path to a successful project.

Reference: "*A Guide to the Project Management Body of Knowledge*" Fourth Edition, or contact me at www.journeyconsulting.org.

Chapter 3

Spiritual Wisdom

Live and Learn

Spiritual Wisdom

"Our greatest problem is not the mistakes we make in life, but that we fail to learn from them."

— *Chuck Swindoll*

Our greatest times of learning come during those seasons of difficulty and times of frustration.

Although not as easy as this may sound, I encourage you to take the high road during challenging times and ask yourself this question:

"What is it that I should be learning from this situation?" God reminds us that difficulties will come, and we should seek His wisdom and look for the learning.

I often bump into the "self-pity trap" but have learned to work hard to push through the challenge and search for what I need to learn.

"Consider it a sheer gift, friends, when tests and challenges come at you from all sides. You know that under pressure, your faith-life is forced into the open and shows its true colors. So don't try to get out of anything prematurely. Let it do its work so you become mature and well-developed, not deficient in any way."

James 1:2-4 The Message

Spiritual Wisdom

Applied Project/Program Management

"Live and Learn"

One of my mantras is "Hope for the best but prepare for the worst" ("live and learn"). Although not the textbook definition, it sure sounds a lot like Risk Management. We benefit from learning both in good and trying times. In addition, what we have lived through on our projects has given us learning opportunities we can apply to our project scenarios. Experience tells us the Risk Management knowledge area is a lot about leveraging our influence as well as learning from our past.

Let's not make that "rookie" PM mistake and ignore managing risks throughout our project process, starting in initiating. Try this, build your plan and execute:

Develop Your Risk Plan: With your team and key stakeholder(s), determine their input on your risk management plan and how you will manage risk. Then build your plan and share it with the entire team.

Identify Risks: Use a simple spreadsheet, or you can develop a risk register. Get your best people in the room and brainstorm and document risks. Or you may want to interview other PMs and experts.

Qualify and Quantify Prioritized Risks: Now that you have your list of risks, rank those risks using a risk-rating matrix to determine high, medium or low risks. Determine the top risks using a numerical quantification.

Plan Your Risk Responses: In this step make sure you have a risk owner and then determine the strategies you will use. Will you accept the risk, mitigate, and/or transfer each risk?

Monitor and Control Risks: Work hard to make sure you pay attention to managing risks based on your plan.

Check out the *Project Management Body of Knowledge* (PMBOK®) or dive into the book *Risk Management — Tricks of the Trade* by best-selling author, Rita Mulcahy, PMP.

Big Ears

Spiritual Wisdom

"Wisdom is the reward you get for a lifetime of listening when you'd have preferred to talk."

— *Doug Larson*

"Big ears" is a term I use when someone speaks and provides us with valuable information or words of wisdom. I like to have "big ears" to listen carefully to every word and catch all the details.

In my life, I have gained a great deal from the guidance and wisdom gained by listening to what I call a "whisper" from God. I have heard this referred to as a "the little voice".

If you hear the "God whisper", I encourage you too to listen carefully and respond. All of us can experience this and gain insight and wisdom. If you haven't heard Him in a while, get really "big ears" to listen.

"Now then, my sons, listen to me and do not depart from the words of my mouth."

Proverbs 5:7 NASB

Spiritual Wisdom

Applied Project/Program Management

"Big Ears"

Yes, I call it the "God whisper". Maybe it's something different for you. Your conscience, the little voice inside your head, or maybe it's just a gut feeling. We can choose for ourselves, but lets all agree that we hear some kind of prompting, and yes, it's very personal.

As we lead projects/programs we are often challenged with finding new ways to handle difficult situations. A paralyzed economy can offer its trickery with reduced budgets and a lack of resources. Organizational changes and re-focusing corporate direction can also create project barriers we are burdened with moving when leading our projects. We have all faced these kinds of issues, and we are still expected to make tough judgment calls.

There is no trick or secret to making the best decision. Here are three things to consider. If you can do these well, they can assist greatly in your decision-making process.

1. Listen
2. Listen
3. Listen

Listen to what your own experience has taught you. You have earned those stripes.

Listen to those around you. They too have earned it from their experiences.

Listen to the "God whisper" for His timeless wisdom.

Wisdom for Free

Spiritual Wisdom

"By the power of faith every enduring work is accomplished."
— *James Allen*

Often we are successful because we are well prepared. We don't always think in the present; rather, we look downstream in order to make the best decision for what is ahead. Some can lay claim to great forethought, or maybe even a little bit of luck; others lay claim to their faith.

I am not sure about you, but for me, knowing there is a God and trusting in His wisdom has carried me through some extremely tough, life-changing decisions. I can say, the more I trust God, my relationship with Him grows stronger and I gain more confidence in the decisions I need to make.

God promises to give us wisdom. All we need to do is ask for it, it's free.

"For the Lord grants wisdom! From his mouth come knowledge and understanding."

Proverbs 2:6 NLT

Spiritual Wisdom

Applied Project/Program Management

"Wisdom for Free"

We all make a multitude of decisions every day. If you are like me, there are those clunky days when we may stumble through the next decision. Some decisions are quick and easy; we just make them and move on. In tougher times, we call on our leadership circle to help us get through. Then there are those times when we alone are asked to make a rare decision that feels impossible. Most of us have been there at some time. If you haven't experienced this, your day will come. You will have to dig deep into your own psyche, into your very soul to make the best and most responsible decision. It's that one-time decision that could impact a very close friend or an unsuspecting team. In those desperate and challenging moments, many look to their faith for help.

Big faith or small faith, it doesn't matter. What matters is that you reach out to God — nobody else, just you and Him. I can tell you, He is always available, and you'll never have to wait on Him. Or maybe you are still searching. That's great, way to go! If He is who He says He is, there is no wisdom more worthy of your time.

Purest Wisdom

Spiritual Wisdom

"The *BusyLeader* must take time to look for God's direction and then act on it."

— Pat Richie

Wow, what an awesome quote by author Pat Richie from his book entitled *Wisdom for the BusyLeader*.

This is a no brainier, right?

I'm not sure about you, but every time I am faced with a tough challenge, I take a moment to pray and ask God for His wisdom and direction. Never, not one time, has He let me down.

I encourage you to seek His guidance, wait, listen and then act.

"For the Lord gives wisdom, and from His mouth come knowledge and understanding."

Proverbs 3:13 NIV

Spiritual Wisdom

Applied Project/Program Leadership

"Purest Wisdom"

Obviously, we don't know it all. A good friend and fellow project manager recently reminded me of the valuable lesson around seeking wisdom. In supporting a current client our team of project managers meet weekly for a Microsoft Project Server (MSPS) support call. The purpose of this call is to bring our MSPS challenges to the meeting and discuss solutions with the others on the call. I told my friend I was hesitant to bring forward the issues, thinking I may be the only one having a certain difficulty. He said, "Take the opportunity to seek the wisdom of the group, and if you have a question, no doubt many others will have the same or similar issues." He reminded me, "We need to be the example, to be humble and ask the questions." He was so right. The next support call I verbalized two MSPS schedule challenges and the support was overwhelming. Also, others had the same or similar issues, and later I received two notes thanking me for getting the ball rolling.

As project/program managers, I was reminded and we must quickly learn to seek wisdom and direction during the most difficult times — it just makes sense. It could be a challenging moment with a customer or with a project sponsor, or maybe a scheduling issue like I had. It could possibly be a new technology that you may not be familiar with, or a project change that isn't quite clear to you.

As we mature in our leadership, we must surround ourselves with the smartest people we can find and then utilize their expertise and wisdom. Whenever we need information regarding a certain area, don't hesitate to leverage your subject matter expert(s) to gain a better understanding of the best practice(s). Seek assistance from a trusted leader, mentor, or a trusted friend. This will ensure the greatest outcome for your project/program.

Right is Always Right

Spiritual Wisdom

"Honesty is the first chapter in the book of wisdom."
— Thomas Jefferson

When it is all said and done, we know the rules. We don't always like them, but we know what is right and what is wrong — at least I hope we all do.

The greatest leadership book of all time is the Bible, and it has helped me learn what I need to know to lead in my life and in my job. Sure, I make mistakes, all the time, but I have found that His teachings have carried me through some really tough days.

In the Bible, I have seen that God is not vague about His expectations for us to be truthful, trustworthy, and honest. Yes, God has tested me for sure. Yet, what I have found in His Word is that it stands the test of time, and His promises have never failed me.

I know it's not always easy, but we can't waver, even on the toughest days. Trusting His leadings has helped me. He has it all under control, and we can count on it!

"Blessed are those who act justly, who always do what is right."
Psalm 106:3 TNIV

Spiritual Wisdom

Applied Project/Program Leadership

"Right is Always Right"

Have you read the Project Management Institute's Code of Ethics lately? Experience has taught me that knowledge around the fundamentals of ethics is a cornerstone of deeper thought leadership and practice.

Temptations come every day in projects and programs simply based on the nature of the discipline. Things like explaining away a missed deliverable or shortcutting a promised quality measure to meet a deadline. These temptations and decisions in pressure moments will define our ethical character. Let's all bone up on the "Code of Ethics" and don't compromise these ethics on any decision — no matter what it costs us. Remember, this simple wisdom: "Right is always right."

Project Management Institute Code of Ethics: www.pmi.org

Chapter 4

Communication

Get in Front of Your Communication

Communication

"Seek first to understand, then to be understood."
— St. Francis of Assisi

In any organization, no matter what level you are, everyone reports to someone and everyone is accountable to someone. The opportunity and criticality of effective communication is one key to success.

We all gather our communication requirements and execute as a standard practice. You know you can exceed the expectations of your audience by providing what they want and how they want it by keeping your communications clear.

BUT, if you want to stay ahead of your audience, let me suggest this foolproof strategy in the forefront of your communication planning:

Present relevant, important, even critical information to your audience before they even know they need to know it. What I mean is get the information in front of them before it becomes their issue.

If you can do this on a consistent basis, you will meet and exceed expectations and stay ahead of your audience every time.

"The wise in heart are called discerning, and gracious words promote instruction."
Proverbs 16:21 TNIV

Communication

Applied Project/Program Management

"Get in Front of Your Communication"

One day I had a discussion with a very bright, but less experienced project manager. He was having difficulty with his current stakeholders. He said, "They don't seem to get it. I keep giving them the information and they keep telling me that over the last few months I am not doing a good enough job communicating with them. What is their problem?" He went on to tell me, "I do a great job getting information to them, but nothing ever seems to be good enough. I'm just going to keep sending my updates and eventually they should be fine." When he concluded, it was obvious to me that the customer was not having a communication issue, but rather this project manager was. The tip off was simple, *having a communication issue "over the last few months..."* YIKES!

Even a simple communication issue should be dealt with within hours, and this scenario went on for a few months. This was an obvious opportunity for a "coachable" moment.

Here are the pointers I shared with him that day: First, as project managers we need to own the issue, this is where it all begins. I don't subscribe to the "customer is always right" philosophy, but when things go off track, we need to start by looking at ourselves in the preverbal "project mirror". Second, sending the same information that hasn't worked in a few months would be like poking a sharp stick in your customer's eye. Doing the same, ineffective step over and over again is like Einstein's definition of insanity. We need to take a **different** course of action. Set up a formal meeting with the customer and own up to the simple fact that *WE* have not met *THEIR* expectations for effective communications. Discuss their communication requirements in terms of *what* they want, *how* they want it, *when* they want it. In addition, be certain before we leave the meeting that we *all* actually agree on what was agreed. When we get back to our desk, send an email thanking them for the meeting and reiterate what was agreed in the meeting. However, we are still not done. Document requirements in the communication plan and set up a meeting with the customer in one week to make sure we are continuing on target and ensure that the customer is satisfied with the new approach to foster good communications. Don't forget, 90% of project and program management is communication — we need to own it!

The 800-Pound Gorilla

Communication

"In life, what you resist persists."

— Werner Erhard

"The 800-pound gorilla." "The elephant in the room." These are common sayings used when dealing with problems and issues.

Although leaders are aware of issues, far too often they shrug them off with hopes these problems will fade into the sunset. Truth be told, they won't and don't. We need to get past the fear of confronting and dealing with problems and place the issue on the table to work it through. Most of us do not like confrontation — I don't — but the fact is, problems need to be resolved because they will not go away on their own, they will only get bigger.

A calm discussion to face a tough issue will often yield a positive result. Not dealing with the issue yields no result and bad consequences later.

When you see that "800-pound gorilla", don't pretend that it isn't there. Talk about it and work to bring the problem to closure.

"No discipline is enjoyable while it is happening — it's painful! But afterward there will be a peaceful harvest of right living for those who are trained in this way."

Hebrews 12:11 HCSB

Communication

Applied Project/Program Management

"The 800-Pound Gorilla"

When speaking with a group of project and program managers about problem resolution, I observed a trend. When engaged in confrontation or conflict with team members, based on issues like late deliverables or poor communication for example, these PMs admitted to choosing "smoothing" tactics, or worse "withdrawal" as their primary resolution strategy. That would be the equivalent of putting a Band-Aid on a deep laceration rather than stitching it up so it can heal without problems arising later. Digging deeper into the discussion it became clear that the pace and workload of these busy leaders created this reckless and ineffective problem-solving tactic.

I coached this team to abandon "withdrawal" and "smoothing" as their primary tactics for problem resolution and instead solve the problem through confrontation. PMI® would tell us that the most effective way to handle problems or issues is through well-disciplined confrontation, and I couldn't agree more. Problems won't simply go away over time if they are ignored; in fact, they will more than likely get worse. When we develop our Project Human Resource Management plan, we must include developing expectations for ways the project team should behave in the area of handling conflict and solving problems. This simple strategy has served me and my project teams well. I would encourage you to build this into your HR strategy. If a problem develops between two individuals, coach them to follow these three simple steps:

1. The person that has the problem should not "sit" on the problem, but rather set up a private meeting immediately with the other to *calmly* discuss it toward a hopeful outcome.

2. If this does not resolve the problem, a second meeting should be set up with these two individuals and the project manager to discuss the problem together and come to closure. Most often, the three of you will come to a resolution or the PM will be the tiebreaker on a decision that needs to be made.

3. If a further step is warranted, set up one final meeting and bring in a trusted leader to bring about an unbiased approach toward problem resolution and closure between the three of you.

The Fifteen-Minute Meeting

Communication

"If there is any great secret of success in life, it lies in the ability to put yourself in the other person's place and to see things from his point of view — as well as your own."

— Henry Ford

The company where I have worked for over eleven years has an interesting way to engage people in their next work assignment. Meaning, we must interview for our next project or role within the company. It does bring variety, and I have been successful growing my career in this type of environment, yet admittedly it is at times stressful. Thus, the "fifteen-minute meeting" story.

I recently was sent a meeting notice from an account director to attend a fifteen-minute meeting. In the subject line it said "Discussion". No real information regarding the essence of the meeting was given, but my gut told me it would be bad news, and I was right. In short, I was told that the account could no longer support the cost of the program I was leading and steps were being taken to "ratchet it down." From a business perspective, this was likely a necessary financial move as this particular account was losing momentum and sales with the customer. Certainly it wasn't personal, but it did feel a bit abrupt and uncomfortable. Sometimes as leaders we may want to consider working to soften the blow of bad news and increase learning for those involved. It could be as simple as bringing our leaders or teams up to speed ahead of the consequence. Maybe bring in the leader and/or team members through the decision-making process so everyone can see the bigger picture. Change is not typically an easy thing for most. If we can dignify the action with the highest level of trust and respect for everyone receiving the hard news, it can soften the blow no matter how difficult the news. People may not always remember everything you did, but they will, however, remember *how* you treated them.

"Careless words stab like a sword, but wise words bring healing."

Proverbs 12:18 NCV

Communication

Applied Project/Program Management

"The Fifteen-Minute Meeting"

We know it, we live it, projects and programs have peaks and valleys, good news and bad news. How we handle both is a critical component of what we do, and it will shape our success or highlight the failure. Giving good news is easy, and for most of us intuitive and enjoyable. In fact, delivering good project news just feels good. Let's be honest, every project suffers setbacks no matter how hard we plan or how good we are. There are too many variables that influence our projects. It could be risks, issues, constraints, known unknowns, and/or unknown unknowns. Maybe we have a challenging customer, unavailable resources, a challenging team member or a drastic decision to terminate the project. Whatever it is, we all know, it will challenge our resolve, impact our project, but mostly it will play on people's emotions. But if we take to heart a couple of simple communication guidelines, we may be able to calm many of those challenges.

- Start by putting yourself in that mental place and accept you will have tough challenges and difficult decisions to make. Often, simply accepting this fact will prepare you for action.

- Try to keep your team ahead of the consequences of bad news. Meaning, as you anticipate a challenge ahead, talk with your team in anticipation of it (much like managing risk).

- Remember, bad news *NEVER* gets better over time; in fact, it gets worse, so don't wait to deliver it. Be reminded that difficult news often comes with difficult consequences so deliver it with compassion. We are all different and we all internalize and process information differently. What may seem small to you could be huge for the person next to you.

- Be completely honest in your delivery and stick to the facts.

- Make certain you answer every single question your team has and make time after the meeting for more private and personal questions.

- This is not an exhaustive list. If we can keep to these foundational guidelines, it can assist in making tough communications a little easier to deliver and for those on our teams to swallow.

Chapter 5

Balance

The Teeter Tauter

Balance

"At times, it is difficult to keep a proper balance in our lives. But, over time, an improper balance will lead to problems."

— Catherine Pulsifer

How's your pace? Have you assessed your work life balance? Recently, my wife and I were marveling at the blessing of growth in our PM consulting practice, but we were reminded that growth comes at a cost. Although we are enjoying our success, the cost to us is that we have less time together, working weekends and late evenings developing and preparing curriculum. Moving into the New Year we are challenging ourselves to continue to assess our balance and make any necessary and appropriate changes to maintain a good balance and enhance our quality of life together. I invite you to take the same challenge.

"After the apostles returned to Jesus, they told him everything they had done and taught. But so many people were coming and going that Jesus and the apostles did not even have a chance to eat. Then Jesus said, 'Let's go to a place where we can be alone and get some rest.'"

Mark 6:30-31 CEV

Balance

Applied Project/Program Leadership

"The Teeter Tauter"

We hear it all the time... "get ur done ...and fast." We are hearing this today more than ever before: "Rapid deployment; crash, fast track your projects, etc."

But where is the balance?

I recently read a note from a respected CEO who, like most, is working diligently to create as much efficiency as possible, and her message was clear. "If there are any processes you are using that aren't adding value for the customer, then stop using them... NOW."

In our fast-paced, high-pressure discipline, companies seem obsessed with a "better, faster, cheaper" mentality. Project/program managers are the victims of this obsession, and often there is no escaping it... or is there? We know the value project/program management brings to any organization with proven processes and procedures that are time tested. Also, I have seen processes executed that do not bring the customer value, or templates leveraged that require information that may not be necessary for the project. Inevitability, it all comes down to balance.

Try this: First, balance by not cutting corners in the heat of the moment or compromising the value we can bring to our customers. Don't add process for the sake of process, but maintain a good balance that adds value. When senior leadership starts pushing the "get-ur-done" button, use your knowledge and influence to assist them in understanding impacts to the triple constraint (scope, time, cost) and propose solutions to maintain a stable project balance. However, don't argue your points without the facts.

Ultimately, it's on us. We are responsible and accountable for maintaining project integrity throughout the project process. Leverage your leadership spirit and yield the maximum result!

Pace Yourself for the Long Haul
Balance

"Every now and then go away, have a little relaxation, for when you come back to your work your judgment will be surer."

— Leonardo Da Vinci

Try this: Take a jar and fill it with stones until you can't add anymore. You can see the jar is full. Pick it up and you will feel its heaviness.

As leaders, sometimes our lives can feel the same — full and heavy. You may feel like you can't add another thing. If this describes you, take heart, you are not alone.

Now try this: Take a cup of sand and slowly pour it into your jar filled with stones. You will quickly see the sand fill in the gaps around the stones. Imagine with me if you will that the sand represents the good stuff in our lives like time off or recognition for a job well done just to mention a few good things. You can see there is still room for these things.

Now take it one step further and remove a bunch of the stones from your jar to lighten your load. You can quickly see that this creates more space for good stuff.

I encourage you as a leader to pace yourself for the long haul. Watch out that you don't jam your jar too full of stones. Make smarter decisions by establishing healthy boundaries so you can have room in your life for the good things.

"For in six days the Lord made heaven and earth, but he rested on the seventh day and was refreshed."

Exodus 31:17 NLT

Balance

Applied Project/Program Leadership

"Pace You for the Long Haul"

I had an opportunity to take a vacation day to Cedar Point in Sandusky, Ohio. Some would say it's the roller coaster capital of the US. I rode many of the roller coasters that day, but the one that was most intimidating for me was the one they call "Maverick". That roller coaster took me from zero to sixty mph in moments with overwhelming inverted twists and turns, loops, up, down and when it was over I was literally physically fatigued.

At times, leadership is much like the Maverick roller coaster. It has those quick turns and up-and-down moments when you can feel like you are going sixty mph. Imagine if you rode the Maverick over and over again with no break. In short order you would feel exhausted, beat up, pushed around and most likely physically sick.

We need to be cautious to not get strapped into the "leadership roller coaster" going from zero to sixty mph with no stops, recovery breaks, or time off.

I encourage you to plan now how you and those on your team will pace and recover. You need to schedule recovery breaks throughout the day. It could be as simple as five minutes every hour, a half or full day team activity, or even well-deserved time off. Replenishing yourself and your team in the short term will yield greater effectiveness in the long term.

Don't burn out... pace yourself and your team for the long haul.

Start-up is Nothing Short of Critical
Balance

"You must master your time rather than becoming a slave to the constant flow of events and demands on your time. And you must organize your life to achieve balance, harmony, and inner peace."

— *Brian Tracy*

Every day we face the challenge and make choices to balance our life and our work. This is one of our more challenging areas of leadership — yet we own it just the same. We must be diligent to manage our work schedule as well as our home life schedule.

As part of leadership, we have the added responsibility to influence our team regarding their work/life balance. Meaning we need to be acutely aware of the time and schedule pressures we are imposing on each member of our team(s) from the get-go. We want our people to have time with their families and keep balance in their work and home life. This is not an easy task for sure, but it is worth our maximum effort. We need to set the tone for the team early on.

Think about it. Your organization, project or program could be known as the functional team with functional families, and people are clamoring to work with you.

"There's an opportune time to do things, a right time for everything on the earth."

Ecclesiastes 3:1 The Message

Balance

Applied Project/Program Management

"Start-up is Nothing Short of Critical"

A successful project is no small task and start-up will be your opportunity to influence a level playing field.

Communicate carefully and be cautious not to make promises or concessions at the expense and consequence of your team. There is a lot to consider, but here are a couple of steps in start-up that need your utmost attention:

- Begin to establish a relationship with key client stakeholders and agree on expectations. Let them know the capabilities of your team, but most of all the importance of developing a "real" schedule in order to maximize resources and minimize defects.
- Develop a comprehensive project charter that will outline the starting point of your project.
- Consider your high-level requirements to get a project snapshot.
- Check your organizational assets. This will give you a grounding of your start-up PM requirements.
- Pull together your contact list. Get those important team members added to your list so when you need to make contact, it is a simple process. Don't forget to maintain your contact list as the project progresses.
- Consider carefully and develop a comprehensive list of constraints with your team and primary stakeholders.
- Carefully determine and then analyze assumptions. Determine how they may impact your project from a qualitative and quantitative standpoint.
- Build your issues/actions and decision log.
- Begin identifying and documenting the obvious risks.

Depending on your own organization, there could be other steps in start-up, but this is a good place to begin.

Cheat Your Employer

Balance

"Balance, peace, and joy are the fruit of a successful life. It starts with recognizing your talents and finding ways to serve others by using them."

— Thomas Kinkade

I bet I got your attention with this title! Of course, I don't mean literally "cheat" your employer. In this context I am referring to our decision to give up one thing in order to gain something else.

Research would tell us that 30% of our waking hours are spent at work. This is a reality for most and acceptable. As many of us know, our time at work can easily bleed over into our personal lives. Many are faced with a decision to spend much more than 30% work time, maybe 50% or 60%, and even worse, a more drastic 70%. This is sad but true and leaves us unbalanced and missing out on time at home.

In our one and only life, let's consider the consequences of an unbalanced work and home life for ourselves, our family and our team. Certainly, due to a variety of circumstances there are seasons when work demands a longer day, week or even a month. But this should be the *exception* and not the norm. However, for many this is tough to discern. So think about choosing to cheat your employer (balance or give up those long hours) in order to gain more time at home.

Remember, do "everything in moderation". We hear this all the time, as too much of one thing drastically impacts the other. The "balance dance" can be challenging, but all of us need to be mindful to not tip the scale in either direction.

"It is useless for you to work so hard from early morning until late at night, anxiously working for food to eat; for God gives rest to his loved ones."

Psalm 127:2 NLT

Balance

Applied Project/Program Management

"Cheat Your Employer"

One rare Saturday morning I was flipping through cable channels to catch up on the week's latest news and stumbled upon a political roundtable debate. I would typically pass it by, but this time it grabbed my attention because the debate was focused on a decision that a top government official had made based on a campaign promise. The problem was that one decision was a date-driven ultimatum without understanding the breath of the consequences. In PM terms, the decision maker didn't fully understand the scope, and the decision he made didn't allow the primary stakeholders to weigh in on the impacts of his date-driven ultimatum prior to making the decision. Now, of course, everyone is backpedaling, debating, arguing and scratching their heads on how they will get this project completed and to what consequence. Sound familiar? Obviously, this is a perfect argument for making sure we include and listen to our stakeholders before we or anyone else makes project decisions. However, I would like to shift the focus to "our" responsibility as project/program influencers. In reality, we are sometimes given date constraints that may be unshakable. I get that. Yet we still have the responsibility to not just "sit on our hands" and accept a bad decision and throw our balance out of whack. Rather, we must articulate to the sponsor/leadership how their decision can impact much more than *they* are even aware of, so our influence is key to:

- Gather the facts;
- Look at historical data;
- Meet with the project team leaders;
- Take the time to discern and understand everything that needs to occur to meet the imposed deadline;
- Maintain high quality; and
- A healthy balance in your own life as well as the lives of those on your team.

This could mean breaking the project into phases or minimizing the scope. Maybe it's a more comprehensive risk management strategy. It should never mean selling out your team to work seventy hours a week for the next year and a half. Take your argument to the sponsor/leadership and negotiate utilizing the facts. Most often a compromise can be rendered on both sides of the argument. Nobody wants to work on a *death march* project — least of all your teammates.

What Color is Your Flag?
Balance

"Live a balanced life — learn some and think some and draw and paint and sing and dance and play and work every day some."

— Robert Fulghum

I had a quick call the other day with my oldest son Pete at the end of what he described as a "very long and grueling day." He was hoping to leave by 5:00 p.m., but at 6:45 p.m. he was still finishing some critical tasks in his office and missing out on a barbeque with friends. He said, "Dad, it's really hard to get it all done in a day with everything I need to do at work and at home." His comment is something we can all relate to in our own lives.

Yet, we get things done and most often we do it well, in fact, it is the inherent nature of our role and how we are wired as leaders. But that doesn't mean it's easy.

When work *naturally* spills over into our personal life, or worse, every area of our life, the yellow flag of caution should be raised. This is the time we must look diligently at all areas of our life before the yellow flag of caution turns into the red flag of danger.

"I have seen what is best for people here on earth. They should eat and drink and enjoy their work, because the life God has given them on earth is short."

Ecclesiastes 5:18 NCV

Balance

Applied Project/Program Management

"What Color is Your Flag?"

As mentioned earlier, one characteristic of the company where I work is that when a project ends we have to interview inside the company for our next position. With the assistance of our manager, we search every area of the company for our next assignment. We look at our options, express our interest(s), and based on those options we interview for the role. For me, I like the variety, but often it is a bittersweet transition. It can be stressful but also somewhat exciting just the same.

In my recent transition, I had two great opportunities to choose from — two interviews and one choice to make. One role combined a high-profile program opportunity in an account and a "shared" project leadership role in another, very different account. I learned during the interview that this option was a highly visible "progressive" option, which is code for "chaotic and risky". The other less visible role offered its own significant and unique challenges to lead a virtual, global project team. It was a complementary project to coincide with another more visible project that was far along its project path. One forte I always lay claim to is that I bring calm to chaos, so the first option felt a bit more appealing to me, yet I could see a "red flag of chaos" in the foreground. I had a few days to consider and make my decision because, just like you, my work is important to me.

I worked through my thought process considering *ALL* the areas of my life and how this decision will impact and influence the next eighteen months. I considered the impacts on my family and friends. I prayed about my decision, spoke in-depth with my wife and family, met with my boss and quickly my choice became abundantly clear.

This time I chose the "green flag of calm" over the "red flag of chaos". I chose less visibility and lower profile in a virtual role over the other option. This choice will allow me a healthier balance to honor every area of my life over the next eighteen months.

When it's your turn, what will you choose?

Chapter 6

Character

The Gloom and Doomer

Character

"The next step in building a dream team is to establish clear criterion for the selection of specific team members. Character. Competence. Chemistry."

— Bill Hybels

The buck stops with us, so we must be diligent to choose the right people for our teams. I once worked with a very capable colleague who was smart, talented, and gifted at her trade. She had many virtues and leveraged those to accomplish some really great work. However, she had one vice that created an unbalanced challenge for me almost daily. I call it the "gloom and doom" syndrome. I loved the ability she had, but often I felt dragged down by her "downer desperation".

We don't always have this luxury, but as often as we can, surround yourself with individuals who are not only competent and loaded with character but also bring a replenishing professionalism to the mix of the team.

Never underestimate the importance of team chemistry.

"They must first be tested; and then if there is nothing against them, let them serve as deacons."

1 Timothy 3:10 TNIV

Character

Applied Project/Program Leadership

"The Gloom and Doomer"

I attended a leadership conference and learned an extraordinary way to select the best people for my team. It is a simple, yet high-powered formula called the "3-Cs": c̲haracter, c̲ompetence and c̲hemistry. Start with character. Know who you are choosing for your team, as this drives the other two "Cs". This person will be an extension of your team and will influence your project/program.

I recall I once gave permission to a young, talented developer to work from home, as he needed to do this. Often, team members or I would try to contact him, but he never seemed to be available. After a few incidents, I confronted him and he became aggressively defensive. I explained to him a simple, legitimate explanation could have solved this issue quite easily. His defensive posture raised a big "red flag" for me and others. This led me to question his character, and in time he was moved on.

Whenever we bring someone onto our team, certainly we review their resume and credentials, but keep in mind that everyone typically looks good on paper. If he/she is internal to your company, talk with their former leaders about their work ethic. Interview the candidate by asking behavioral type questions, like how they might handle certain situations with others and even yourself. Dig deep and don't be shy about it. An individual who lacks character can crush your team dynamic, challenge your leadership, and jeopardize your project/program. Maybe even your organization.

Don't ever settle.

Right or Privilege
Character

"Attitude is a little thing that makes a big difference."

— Winston Churchill

My philosophy about having a job has changed over the years. I used to believe it was my right to be employed. Wow, was I ever wrong! We are all given specific abilities and talents. It is clearly a privilege to use those abilities and talents in a job where we can impact others and excel at whatever we choose to do.

Our attitude and how we handle this privilege can make all the difference in our work and to everyone around us.

"And whatever you do or say, do it as a representative of the Lord Jesus, giving thanks through him to God the Father."

Colossians 3:17 NLT

Character

Applied Project/Program Management

"Right or Privilege"

I have found quite conclusively that each role on our project teams has its own significance, and we mustn't forget that.

Some roles have a greater visibility in the foreground, like your Technical Lead or Subject Matter Expert. Others like a Level 1 Developer or a Project Coordinator may be in the background or behind the scenes.

Over the years I have learned quickly to treat all individuals with equal importance regardless of their role or level of responsibility.

Lessening the importance of one's role or responsibility or even one person's contribution can be devastating to a team and an individual. If we as leaders de-value a team member AND/OR the team, it will send a clear message to everyone that it is OK. It also gives them permission to do the same.

Pay attention. Be consistent and let's make every effort to know and understand the unique value every member contributes to the project as a whole. Honor each person no matter how big or small their contribution may seem.

Have Their Back

Character

"If you truly know and care for the people entrusted to your leadership, they will instinctively take care of the mission, one another and their leader. But none of this will be possible until you know your people."

— *Commentary by Capt. Marcos Baca 386th Expeditionary Force Support Squadron Deputy Commander United States Air Force.*

Leading is a tough gig, and staying organized always has its challenges. Let's keep this in the forefront of our mind: Take the greatest care of our people we can. No really, make this our first priority. It seems fundamental but often in our hectic work patterns other things seem to become a higher priority. Build trust, show unending respect, keep our people dignified, always have their back and lead with all diligence. They will respect you despite the circumstance. Remember the old adage: "If you lead and no one follows, you are simply taking a walk."

"I am the good shepherd; I know my sheep and my sheep know me."

John 10:14 TNIV

Character

Applied Project/Program Leadership

"Have Their Back"

Getting your project/program team on board with you, your vision, your goals and objectives is way harder than hoping it happens. Good advice, start every project/program with your people as the highest priority.

You need to know *your* people. In the earliest phases of your project make time to sit down one-on-one with each team member, talk with them and get to know them. I didn't say talk at them; a robot can be programmed to ask the right questions. We must ask those more personal questions with the right heart or people will see right through us. This isn't the time to interview them or tell them your expectations. "People don't care how much you know until they see how much you care." This is that precious "first time" you really get to know them. Don't squander it!

Find out who they are and what they like. Ask them what passionately drives them. Get to know the names of their kids, what grade they are in, and what activities they are involved in. Talk to your team members about their hobbies so you can have conversations with them maybe when they return from a long weekend, in the hall, or at the opening or close of a meeting.

Know *your* people. People are *not* motivated by *our* needs but by their needs.

Remember, they work so they can have a life, NOT the opposite.

Less is More

Character

"To know you have enough is to be rich."
— Lao-Tzu, Tao Te Ching

In previous years, my part-time evening job with our small consulting business has been doing very well. It has allowed us the opportunity to pay down debt and manage our money more wisely. Yet it has also tempted us to be frivolous and desire to purchase "things" we "want" but do not really need.

Jesus Christ, whom I believe is the greatest leader of all time, often reminds us not to wrap ourselves around what we own because these things are not eternal. He doesn't say we can't have nice "things", just don't make those "things" and money what we worship.

We are not who we are because of how much we have, but rather by our character and example.

"Rich people may think they are wise, but a poor person with discernment can see right through them."

Proverbs 28:11 NLT

Character

Applied Project/Program Management

"Less is More"

It doesn't take long to learn that sometimes less can be more. In project leadership we strive to give our customers the best service which will lead to a great project outcome. However, if we skew from our plan, we could find ourselves off target by adding un-asked-for extras and impacting our project negatively.

Research suggests that gold plating* can kill our project/program. Early on in my project management career, I fell into what I call the "customer is always right" trap. I was given a small project and I planned my scope well — or so I thought. However, I allowed myself to accept multiple changes from the customer. I thought it would please them, and it would also allow my employer to make more money from the additional updates. As you may have anticipated, my thinking was not wise. My inexperience as a PM, coupled with not following a change-control process to ensure all changes were documented and managed through that process led to significant problems with the customer. Even worse, we were three weeks late on our deliverable and $20K over budget. When it was all said and done, I had an unhappy sponsor. Certainly, this was not my best project. The upside was an invaluable learning experience through several hard-learned lessons.

We all work hard to develop a solid plan to manage our projects, but we must not let our emotions and personal needs get in the way of providing rock-solid leadership and good PM practices. Clearly in this scenario less was certainly more.

Stick to your project plan and set change-control expectations upfront with your stakeholder(s). Always keep in mind how a lack of judgment and flawed project leadership cannot only impact the *triple constraint but our leadership credibility as well. I encourage everyone to not make the same mistakes that I did.

*Gold plating: Giving customers extras. Gold plating does not add value to the project.

Resist and Run

Character

"Good habits result from resisting temptation."

Ancient Proverb

Wegmans is a very large grocery store chain headquartered in Rochester, New York. Whenever I am in the store, I am faced with their enormous selection of food. Literally, they offer anything you could ever want to eat... anything. I have always had to watch what I eat, but I have this overwhelming temptation to grab a Nutty Bar or a Devil Dog instead of the delicious fresh fruit I should be eating. And nobody would ever know that I chose unwisely, only me. This is one of dozens of temptations we all face on a daily basis.

When temptations nag at us, just WALK, NO RUN AWAY... there is always a way out. Don't rationalize it, resist and run!

"Happy is the man who doesn't give in and do wrong when he is tempted, for afterwards he will get as his reward the crown of life that God has promised those who love Him."

James 1:12 TLB

Character

Applied Project/Program Management

"Resist and Run"

Projects: Unique, temporary and progressively elaborated. That definition alone can suggest complexities we face in projects/programs. Complexities lead to decisions and consequences for completed or missed deliverables.

We do face pressure while managing our projects, and with that pressure comes temptation. We have temptations to maybe skip a step in a process or misrepresent a status to satisfy a sponsor or client. We may find ourselves taking credit for something someone else did or even giving only half the truth on the state of a deliverable in trouble.

Leaders must always hold themselves to a higher personal level of accountability. We can't expect those we lead to resist these temptations if we don't.

People *are* watching us — even when we are not aware that they are — we cannot let them down. Do the right thing and remember: "Right is always right!"

Kill Them with Kindness
Character

"Don't wait for people to be friendly, show them how."

— Unknown

The Background: I have worked at a leading global technology services Fortune 500 Company for over a decade. Upon being hired, I traveled almost full time for the first year. I remember being overwhelmed with an enormous amount of new corporate processes, and I needed to complete dozens of administrative tasks that were complex and cumbersome. They had an unfriendly, bulky, time-tracking tool with hourly reporting on individual tasks; an expense report process that took literally hours to figure out and even longer to track expenses on multiple levels with many forms, copies and reports to complete, just to name a few. And, at that time, they provided administrative support for new employees. Our company had Administrative Assistants to render support for new employees to help them get up-to-speed on all these corporate processes and procedures. These "Admins" supported dozens of employees, and although their job was very busy, it was made clear to me that I was to ask and I would receive support to deliver all these administrative tasks on time as required.

The Issue: The problem, however, was that the Admin assigned to support me was just wicked to work with. In fact, she was downright mean. As I was the new kid on the block, she was aggressive and disrespectful to say the least. Like most new hires, I initially had dozens of questions, and she was far less than accommodating, but I was still on the hook to get my administrative tasks completed in a timely fashion. This Admin made this extremely hard and stressful.

My Strategy: I took the high road. In my dealings with her I chose to approach each interchange in a positive way and to "kill her with kindness", so to speak, regardless of the way she responded to me. In that same vein, it was quite obvious I would need to verbally confront the situation with her in the near term as well as escalate the situation to my leadership. She and I continued to have dozens of interchanges, mostly through email and several by phone, and, believe me, they were brutal. Each email I sent was carefully crafted, respectful and courteous regarding every question I asked, and I responded to her emails in the same way. I have always made it a practice to work hard to be kind in all my communications, but this situation needed some extra attention. A feature of Microsoft

Outlook saves every email that is sent, so I created a folder just for her email responses. I dialogued and documented all of our verbal conversations with the date, time stamp, and the details of our discussion. Furthermore, after each verbal conversation I would follow-up with an email to validate the points we discussed. I kept this strategy up for the better part of a month as I prepared to confront and escalate this situation.

The Consequence: Before I could escalate, I received a meeting request from my leader regarding my interchanges with this Admin. I shared with my leader each scenario and all the emails and documentation I had compiled. I found out shortly thereafter that the Admin was terminated — an unfortunate consequence for her. Although it was never revealed to me, I knew there must have been dozens of other issues raised and not just those that she had with me.

The Lesson and Learning: I am sharing this story with you because of the valuable lessons I learned and live by. My leader told me that if I had chosen a different course of action or approach in my handling of this situation, i.e., like telling her off, sending attacking emails, or raising my voice to her, this could have very well jeopardized my employment. Instead, my leader praised me for practicing great restraint and for my professionalism. At that time I was also reminded to bring the issue up much earlier; however, she understood my hesitancy as the new kid on the block and my desire not to be a squeaky wheel. An excellent lesson! I would *never* suggest that you be someone's doormat, but in this situation and many since, I have learned that challenging rudeness with rudeness will most times escalate an already volatile situation into one that is much worse — a lose/lose scenario for everyone!

When we all look back on our own delicate and challenging interchanges, and as we even look ahead at the next, can we say with confidence we showed or will show great restraint to yield the best result by **"killing them with kindness?"**

Truth and Consequences
Character

"We seek the truth and will endure the consequences."
— Charles Seymour

At one time I was asked to serve in a leadership role for a not-for-profit organization alongside some really good people. This organization had lost two key leaders in a short, six-month timeframe, and they asked me to provide leadership support. The role required both a deep dive into the belly of the organization and to make recommendations on some needed changes. From the outside, many thought it was a healthy organization. Yet, as I looked deeper, what I found was much different. Sadly, what I discovered was a well-intentioned volunteer group of overseers/board members functioning in a grossly dysfunctional way. As I uncovered the hidden truths, I was saddened and at times defeated. But I was diligent although it was painful to factually report my findings and recommendations.

As leaders, it is easy to speak to the smaller, less serious issues and problems. It is those difficult, challenging, and sometimes-painful realities that must be communicated regardless of the circumstance or the consequence. We have the responsibility to make sound decisions based on factual information and to communicate our findings to the appropriate audience. In essence, we are truth-tellers even when it does not feel or look good.

The consequence of difficult truth telling is hard but never wrong, and it often renders the greatest result.

"In the end, people appreciate honest criticism far more than flattery."

Proverbs 28:23 NLT

Character

Applied Project/Program Management

"Truth and Consequences"

It is natural to lean toward our area of strength — the things we are good at. Equally, we respond and react to those things that are easily solved and quickly controlled. Yet, in the heat of battle when projects get a bit ugly — and we all have those moments — have we paused to consider our ability and capability for handling the delicate moments? You know what I mean... those moments when every leadership bone in your body tells you to confront a difficult circumstance. We know if we do this, it could have consequences for you and your project. We have all been there. Like many, I have had to deliver a performance report to someone that has been performing poorly, and I needed to put them on an improvement plan. Another time I had to take away a corporate credit card from an employee using it for personal reasons. Yet another, I challenged a team member who was knowingly padding an estimate so they could make themselves and the project look good — these are just a few examples of delicate moments.

I am sure many of you have experienced circumstances much like mine, but believe me when I tell you, helping them is not helping them. When we allow individuals to continue consequential behaviors or enable their behavior, we are only escalating the problem rather than solving it. It *will* get worse and *not* get better. You then become part of the problem rather than part of the solution. Sound harsh? Not really. I don't mean that we "hammer" them, but deliver the message to them with consideration and compassion for their circumstances. We need to look at the extenuating conditions that created their issue/challenge and then "assist" them toward a solution. Our ultimate role as their leader is **to make them better employees, better people, regardless of the circumstances.** We should start by looking for the root cause and deal with it to work out a solution in *their* best interest. I have found, and I bet you have too, that most people are inherently good.

Believe it or not, people crave truth-filled discipline *with* compassion and care. In most cases, the bad ones will eventually weed themselves out, or you may have to. Either way, you and those you have caringly touched will benefit. You can count on it.

Old Dog New Tricks
Character

"The ultimate measure of a person is not where they stand in moments of comfort and convenience, but where they stand in times of challenge and controversy."
— Martin Luther King, Jr.

Over the last six-years, I have had the privilege of teaching over five hundred project managers a Project Management Professional® (PMP®) Certification Exam Prep course. I have been fortunate enough to work with so many extraordinary individuals and blessed to have had a 98% pass rate. Each learner worked very hard, and I am proud of all of them.

These diverse groups of learners come from many different industries; some are very skilled and some less, they are young and old, and they do keep me hopping. I had a particular learner, and for this illustration let's call him "Fred". Fred was a bit older than most and an eager engineer type who had been with one company for many years. Fred shared with me that he was "comfortable" in his job, and he really enjoyed it, but his company had been doing projects the same way for several years. Their customers were expecting more of them, so the company made a decision to move ahead of their competitors by placing credentialed project managers on all projects.

Fred and several of his peers enrolled in my ten-week PMP® Certification Exam Prep course. They all worked very hard, especially Fred, as much of the course material was new to him. Fred added a lot of value to class discussions because of his wealth of experience. When his day came to sit for the PMP® Exam, sadly Fred was unsuccessful and did not pass; yet all of his peers did. I reached out to Fred as I learned of his exam fate to encourage him, and I was surprised that he was more of an encouragement to me. Fred explained to me that the journey was a good one and what he did learn in the course he was able to immediately apply to his job. He felt the training made him a better project manager. He showed he was grateful for the opportunity to learn and grow. He was of course disappointed, but not discouraged. His attitude was inspiring, and I was energized by his self-confidence in spite of not passing the exam. (Keep in mind the rigor for exam prep is three months in duration with three and a half hours of class time each week and ten hours study outside of class.)

I am always amazed at the resiliency of those who can bounce back from challenge with an encouraged heart. Fred chose to look at this as his opportunity rather than a letdown. He used his learning as a tool to do his job better, and he held his head high. He didn't cast blame, or whimper — he accepted his circumstance and moved on. This is a great example of victory for the human spirit. I hope Fred helps change your demeanor and outlook in the face of adversity.

OH... by the way, about two months later I got an email from Fred. He worked through our "exam cram plan" and took the PMP® Exam and passed this time. This was great news and I was super excited for him. In the last line of his email he said, ***"I guess you <u>can</u> teach an old dog new tricks."*** WAY TO GO "FRED"! YOU ARE AN INSPIRATION TO US ALL!

Character

Application Project/Program Management

"Old Dog New Tricks"

I love Fred's story, and I pray it encourages you as it did me. But what is the connection to project/program management? I'd be willing to bet we all experience those disappointments or are required to dig into new processes, tools or procedures that sap our time and/or we feel may be unnecessary. Or maybe there is something in your personal life.

I recently found myself frustrated and griping out loud about all the stuff I have to learn because of new customer requirements. Unlike Fred's stellar approach around "opportunity", I fell into the trap that maybe we all fall into by being too "comfortable" for our own good. I realized how ridiculous my griping sounded, "ARE YOU KIDDING ME?" I thought. Here I am in an unbelievable learning opportunity every day, exactly where I prayed to be, and exactly where I should be. And by the way, I am not that much younger than Fred, so just bonk me on the head!

Let me challenge you. Take five short minutes and, in the white space below, jot down an experience you may have or one from your past that now you realize is really a blessing in disguise. Jot it down along with an action or two. I encourage you to not take your challenges for granted. These can be subtle reminders of the blessings we receive disguised as adversity.

Your notes here:

Chapter 7

Relationships

Never Burn a Bridge

Relationships

"The most important single ingredient in the formula of success is knowing how to get along with people."

— *Theodore Roosevelt*

As we settle into our own professional discipline and grow our careers, we will see our network grow as well. It becomes inevitable at different points in our professional life that we will bump into, partner with, or make future contacts with people from our past. Even in the giant, global IT company where I currently work I have come across people five years later on a project that I am asked to lead. Over the years, I also bump into colleagues at seminars, tradeshows, workshops and events.

Throughout our professional lifetime, we never know the direction our life journey may take us and who we may be associated with in the near and distant future.

A mandatory rule to live by is to "never burn a bridge" — never! At the end of the day, it is all about relationships, so keep each one sacred.

"Always be humble and gentle. Be patient with each other, making allowance for each other's faults because of your love. Make every effort to keep yourselves united in the Spirit, binding yourselves together with peace."

Ephesians 4:2-3 NLT

Relationships

Applied Project/Program Management

"Never Burn a Bridge"

Project/program management by its very nature has conflict and confrontation. In fact, it is inevitable. We make dozens of decisions on a daily basis. If you think about it, how we facilitate through those decisions becomes more important than the decision itself, as the outcome will be relational and all decisions impact people. These impacts influence our team members, projects, our own reputation, and how we are seen and treated in the future.

Whether we are in a large or small company or live in a small community, it is likely you will be associated with the same people again over the course of time. People never forget the impression you left with them or how you made them feel.

Our role may require us to negotiate with a zealous spirit, or make a tough leadership decision on a critical deadline or change request, as it is the nature of our work. Project leaders have to deliver information from time to time that may be bad news for the project or those resources serving the project. But we still have the responsibility to tell the full story and the hard truth.

In that delicate moment, we must be critically careful, no matter what the communication is, not to push anyone down in order to lift ourselves up. Even if it is unintentional, the very second that we do, we will jeopardize the trust of every decision thereafter. More importantly, we may have burned a bridge and negatively impacted someone.

You can count on it, if we leave a negative scar, intentional or not, it could come back to haunt us later. It is never too late to perform bridge repair. You'll be glad you did.

The Iceberg Theory

Relationships

"They don't care how much you know until they know how much you care."

— *John C. Maxwell*

In the field of medicine, surgery could be considered the "science" side of medicine, whereas bedside manner is the "art" side. We know that physicians cannot be completely successful if they only treat the disease and ignore the emotional component of a patient. I guess unless you're "Dr. House."

In most cases, 20-40% of an iceberg is above the waterline. Research suggests that leadership is typically broken down into technical skills, the "science" side, and personal/business skills are considered the "art" side. Above the waterline are the technical skills needed. You can see them and they are easy to demonstrate, like performance appraisals, project and training plans, etc.

Conversely, 60-80% of the iceberg is underwater. This would represent the "art" side of leadership. These skills create an environment where leaders communicate effectively within the organization's culture. Ways to motivate and encourage employees, solve problems effectively, make well thought-out and sound decisions. A clear understanding and practice of these skills will enhance the success of an organization and successful projects exponentially.

Application of a well-balanced skill set both above and below the waterline is essential, as human beings are the heart of every organization.

"And let us be concerned about one another in order to promote love and good works."

Hebrews 10:24 HCSB

Relationships

Applied Project/Program Management

"The Iceberg Theory"

Knowing how to apply and understand process, tools and techniques, the "science" side of project management, is important. No one can argue that. However, the bigger piece is the timeless principles of working within the organization where you are impacting those you lead within your project team. Without the "art" side skills to help us define business value, clarify vision, provide direction, build teams or manage conflict, we will not do justice to what our teams and organizations deserve.

True story: As I came onto an account, my manager described the customer I would be working with as "an emotional freight train." In essence, this customer was very demanding, and it was rumored he escorted the last project manager out by the back of his shirt collar. Surely an urban legend... I hoped. Let's call this customer "Joe".

I needed to meet with Joe to begin our relationship, so I scheduled a one-on-one meeting to set expectations. Yes, I was a bit nervous, but I knew if we didn't take the time to begin conversations, it would haunt me later. We were in a small conference room at a table that could only seat two people. He walked in and we exchanged names and handshakes. Before we were both seated he forcefully said: "Steve, I need you to know that the customer is always right." I knew in that moment a quick reactive response could make or break the relationship, so I was slow to answer as I let his comment sink in for a short moment. As we were both seated and both on the edge of our chairs, I took a deep breath, I sat back, and almost in a whisper I responded: "Joe, I don't completely agree, and here is why. I believe the customer believes they are always right and most often for good reason. However, they sometimes don't understand all the circumstances. You hired me to understand all the circumstances, provide advice, and then *together* we make the best decision for the business." I went on to tell him, "It is my responsibility to make sure you receive all the good news *and* the bad news in a timely manner. Any changes on your end, I will expect that you will extend me the same courtesy." Interestingly he didn't agree or disagree —we just moved on to complete the meeting, yet my point was made.

The "art" side of project leadership is most critical to function holistically as a project/program manager. Make it a top priority.

Office Cliques

Relationships

"Treat people as if they were what they ought to be and you help them to become what they are capable of being."
— *Johann Wolfgang von Goethe*

Several years ago, I managed a program team that included a member, well, let's call her "Gail" for this illustration.

Unfortunately, there was a small "clique" within the program team that would brutally complain about Gail over issues ranging from her lack of competence, her awkward personality, but mostly her communication style. This particular team was co-located, which made it easy for me to observe both Gail's behavior and her accusers. As I expected, my observations didn't match what the "clique" of four was reporting. Furthermore, I had set measures for each team member, to include Gail, and her work was always done on time and above expectations. I continued to give Gail stretch, high-profile development activities, much to the objections of the "clique". They did not make it easy for Gail, or for me either. I confronted each member of the "clique" individually and could in fact show them Gail's positive results. But they couldn't get past their negativity. It seemed they just did not like her. Gail struggled every day, and I found myself working hard to continue to encourage and boost her confidence. An interesting side note now several years later, in the midst of these tough economic times, each member of the "clique" has been laid off while Gail is still gainfully employed and quite successful. I am so proud of her!

Encouraging someone and building into their confidence is an incredible opportunity we have as leaders. It can have the potential to change a life. Many will look back and remember when a teacher, mentor, or a leader believed in them, and they can even reflect back to the moment when they started to believe in themselves.

"Finally, brothers and sisters, rejoice! Strive for full restoration, encourage one another, be of one mind, live in peace. And the God of love and peace will be with you."

2 Corinthians 13:11 TNIV

Relationships

Applied Project/Program Management

"Office Cliques"

People's backgrounds and personalities are diverse. Being tolerant of those differences is required and needs to be a core team value for both individuals and a team.

In the *Project Management Body of Knowledge* (PMBOK®) there is a section in the Human Resource knowledge area that makes reference to leadership styles. I am a firm believer that every member of any project/program team has leadership responsibility at some level. In fact, during a former program I asked team members to participate in weekly leadership coaching to look at and discuss different leadership philosophies, tactics, and strategies. It was optional but most attended when they could. This was also a perfect venue to talk about team expectations, get input, buy-in, and to incorporate new leadership strategies. We covered a lot of ground during these coaching sessions, yet one topic rose to the surface: how we were choosing to treat one another.

How we act and interact with one another needs to be agreed upon and articulated clearly. Set team guidelines and expected behaviors. We should not condone judgmental behaviors and/or blatant negative inferences regarding team members. We must act by confronting and not participating in conversations that are detrimental to other team members who are present or absent. Here are three easy strategies to alleviate team murmuring at the water cooler:

- Don't participate by adding negative sentiment to the conversation.
- Be courteous, yet abundantly clear to those involved that the conversation is unacceptable.
- Quickly, and as kindly as possible, simply end the conversation.

The Core of Success

Relationships

"You need to be aware of what others are doing, applaud their efforts, acknowledge their successes, and encourage them in their pursuits. When we all help one another, everybody wins."

— *Jim Stovall*

I recently provided a one-day workshop for a company who is one of "The Rochester, NY Top 100 Companies" as determined by KPMG. The audience was a group of engineers, the training was about project leadership and was entitled *"Creating a Success Revolution"*. In essence, the workshop objective was to improve their *internal* employee morale so it would result in a positive and influential impact on their *internal and external* customer satisfaction. I leveraged successful examples from several corporations, yet one corporation really stood out in my mind... Southwest Airlines. Gary Kelly, CEO, and his Southwest Airline colleagues stressed the importance of building the foundation of their company on their people. They wrapped this philosophy around building relationships of shared goals, shared knowledge and mutual respect. Herb Kelleher, founder of Southwest Airlines says: "There is one key to profitability and stability during a boom or bust economy: employee morale. People are our most valuable asset. Our employees come first. We are only as strong as our people."[1]

Our customers — those we serve — both internally and externally, are the core and the backbone of success for any organization.

"Therefore encourage one another and build each other up, just as in fact you are doing."

1 Thessalonians 5:11 NIV

---

[1] Marketing Innovators: White Paper about Southwest Airlines

Relationships

Applied Project/Program Management

"The Core of Success"

One of our most valuable assets is our team or "internal customer".

We have a lot to think about when managing our projects/programs. Our customers are vast and varied, in and outside of our project boundaries, meaning our internal and external customers. Many don't think of their "project team" as their "customers", but for the sake of this learning example, let's shift to this paradigm.

If you have a seasoned team, or as you begin to work with a new project team, consider these three questions:

- Who are your primary internal customers?
- Are there specific characteristics that differentiate your internal customers from others with whom you work?
- How would you assess your service to these customers?

There are more questions we could ponder, but this should serve as a good baseline or even the start of your own HR Measurement Plan. *Internal* customer satisfaction can face some pretty heavy distractions. These distractions can impact us, our team, and our project. For example: *"I don't like what I do."*

Does *liking* what we do have an impact on what we are capable of, how we treat our peers, or how we are being treated? We can decide based on our own experiences, but my answer is YES! I would contend, and research would validate, that motivation for many can be internally focused. Therefore, we must set up an environment that creates energy and an atmosphere so our internal customers enjoy what they do and participate with a zealous disposition. Here are several suggestions to battle the "I don't like what I do" syndrome:

- Talk with your "internal customer" (team member) and find out what they enjoy doing, and if possible place them in that role and then stretch them.
- Pay attention to them, showing them you care. Really care about what they are doing. Patrick Lencioni, Founder and CEO of The Table Group says: "People who see themselves as invisible, generic or anonymous cannot love their jobs no matter what they are doing."
- Make sure they know that their work makes a big difference and

how their work connects to the greater project/program both short and long term.

- Measure, measure, measure. Leverage your HR Measurement Plan *OR* work specifically with individuals to develop a set of reachable, personal success measures. Yes, it is a little more work for you, but you will receive so much more from them in the long term.

In conclusion, by moving an individual into an area/role/tasks they enjoy, demonstrating that you truly care about them, helping them see how their work impacts the greater good, and then measuring the outcome toward success can foster internal motivation and increase our internal customer's self-worth and positive impact. That's the bottom line here and the key to the success of countless corporations around the globe.

Chapter 8

Excellence

Liar-ship?

Excellence

"Those who are blessed with the most talent don't necessarily outperform everyone else. It's the people with follow-through who excel."

— *Mary Kay Ash*

In a recent engagement I worked for a seasoned accounts director who had an in-depth knowledge of the business, a dynamic personality, high intellect, and he *seemed* quite sincere.

We had a standing meeting every two weeks to discuss the program's status. Our discussions were dynamic, full of life, and in fact we would finish each other's sentences at times. Yet when our discussions ended, his actions over the two weeks never matched his words. After our meetings I always sent an email highlighting our follow-up actions, and when I asked him about those actions he said, "The program is on good path and doesn't really need my immediate attention." Over time I could see he was a really good smart guy with empty promises.

As leaders, we need to be keenly aware that people are looking to us for credibility and consistency. As we expect of our team members, we too must dignify our promises with actions or choose not to make promises we can't follow through on. Anything less is devaluing to each member of our team.

"If a man makes a promise to the Lord or says he will do something special, he must keep his promise. He must do what he said."

Numbers 30:2 NCV

Excellence

Applied Project/Program Management

"Liar-ship"

Read the PMBOK®. Look at your own organizational process assets. There are dozens of processes, procedures, strategies and tactics we must understand and execute in order to manage a project well. To meet project objectives, we are expected to focus mainly on those high-impact areas that can affect a project like scope, time, cost, risk, and schedule to name but a few.

But I want to talk more specifically about an area that can feel less significant for some: **managing action items.** Now, please don't turn the page. I know this may not be your top priority, but I challenge you to treat this as a team development activity throughout the life of the project, and here is why. It is about team members keeping their word and making good on promises you have agreed on.

How many times have we facilitated project meetings and one, maybe two, people on your team *NEVER*, I mean never, complete their action items? It may be no big deal to them, but for those that took their time to complete their assigned actions, they will feel resentment and sometimes anger over the long haul which can drag down pockets of our team. Worse, it is a reflection of poor leadership.

Consider this when managing action items to build into our teams:

- Set process expectations with the team regarding the completion of action items, especially the project manager removing all barriers;
- Confront, in kind, consistent process violators and help them understand why this is important for them and the team;
- Be the example in completing action items; and
- Keep simple metrics for actions completed on time, and then celebrate your successes both as a team and individually.

I know this may seem like common sense, but we must take advantage of *every* opportunity to build into our teams by keeping our project promises.

Bring Our Best to Bear

Excellence

"I do the very best I know how, the very best I can, and I mean to keep on doing so until the end."

— Abraham Lincoln

You have heard the saying "You are your own worst critic." For many that is true, but for others not so much.

I shared a meal recently with a young man in his late twenties. He was telling me about how his sales job was going and he said this:

"My job is good, it's low key, but busy. I sell enough to pay my expenses and a little more."

I remember thinking to myself is this smart, young, talented account executive performing to his full potential? I could barely hold the words in.

You and I have control over one thing... OURSELVES! At the end of the day we need to ask ourselves, did I bring my best to the table today?

"In all the work you are doing, work the best you can. Work as if you were doing it for the Lord, not for people."

Colossians 3:23 NCV

Excellence

Applied Project/Program Management

"Bring Our Best to Bear"

Mondays are my most challenging days. After a weekend, getting back into my routine and work zone mindset takes some extra effort, focus, organizational discipline, and a really good pot of coffee!

Recognizing our vulnerable area(s) creates the opportunity to manage through our own weaknesses and turn these into strengths. Think about it. It's like managing risk. If we have a sense of our own vulnerabilities, we can mitigate them to avoid turning those personal risks into our own issues. For me, one example is knowing that my late afternoons are my least productive time. I am disciplined to schedule my toughest tasks earlier in the day.

As PMs, it is equally important to recognize our own team members' vulnerabilities. The easiest way to understand what these are is to simply ask them. Be open, listen and understand that we all have differences. A quick caution: when having this discussion, let your team member know you are asking about their vulnerabilities so they can be working from their area(s) of strength. Understanding their challenging area(s) will help you be in a better position to assist them. This strategy will also help you balance the project's activities by maximizing your team.

Make this part of your Project Human Resource activities as you develop your project/program team. It's a win/win for everyone!

Execute

Excellence

"Our work is the presentation of our capabilities."
— Johann Wolfgang Von Goethe

Knowing the theories, procedures and practices of project/program management, or any task for that matter, is great; but honestly, it simply isn't enough. Frankly, most anyone can learn these things.

Execution of these practices makes all the difference. Differentiate yourself and work at the highest level of success and never settle for doing just enough.

"Work hard so you can present yourself to God and receive his approval."

2 Timothy 2:15 NLT

Excellence

Applied Project/Program Management

"Execute"

On my journey, I have talked with dozens that often ask how to be successful in project management over the short and long term. My recent PM career has been in the IT industry. Most PMs that I speak with are concerned about working in a technical environment without a technical degree or development background. We may also apply this concern to other industries as well.

There is something to be said for having industry knowledge for sure. However, I find myself in discussions with people that appear to be a bit shortsighted on this issue of IT or industry-specific knowledge. Many fail to realize that project/program management is in fact its own profession and discipline. It is recognized in the professional arena as a discipline worthy of its value. It is credible and offers several global credentials that are acknowledged and respected around the world. As project management professionals we *must* learn the language and have at least a conceptual to mid-range knowledge of the industry where we work. We should surround ourselves with SMEs that will assist us in that knowledge transfer. Don't be discouraged because frankly no one can know it all.

The IT professionals I have worked with are the best at technical solutioning, and many are experts in multiple technologies. I respect and, in fact, I remain in awe of their technical competency. But when it comes to their knowledge and practice of project management, it is not their area of expertise, and neither do I expect it to be. This makes it easy to draw clear professional distinctions and boundaries.

Most of all, I encourage you to go for opportunities in industries where you lack industry-specific knowledge. Just go for it! Don't put up a perceived barrier for yourself. You are a professional project manager, and I do not want you to feel incompetent supporting or desiring to manage a project in an industry that you may need to learn or grow into. We must be zealous experts of the PM discipline and execute flawlessly to earn the respect for the position we hold and the industry that we support.

Add Value Every Day

Excellence

"I found that the men and women who got to the top were those who did the jobs they had in hand, with everything they had of energy and enthusiasm and hard work."

— Harry S. Truman

Do you settle? I mean do you accomplish just enough to get through the day? I would bet we all fall into that trap every once in a while. Maybe it's the day before a long holiday weekend or the afternoon before a two-week vacation.

Great success is accomplished in a variety of ways, yet I believe it comes down to attitude and action to add value to the work we do. As we go through each day, let's ask ourselves: "Am I giving my best effort today?"

"Whatever you do, do well. For when you go to the grave, there will be no work or planning or knowledge or wisdom."

Ecclesiastes 9:10 NLT

Excellence

Applied Project/Program Management

"Add Value Every Day"

We all desire to add the greatest professional value to our work every day. I'm not sure about you, but I have those crazy project days when it feels like the best thing I did was make the next pot of coffee. I hate days like that. I have been running around all day long, but at the end of the day I find myself asking, what just happened?

These types of days could revolve around everyone needing my attention, project/program distractions or fire drills, a resource off task, impending milestone(s) approaching, or a number of other things... but at the end of the day, I just want to leave feeling fulfilled.

If you are like me and find yourself with everything hitting you all at once, try this. Head it off *before* the day spins out of control. When you see it coming, take the important first step and *recognize* it. We have likely seen the signs before, so get out in front of it. Take a brief moment and pause. Really, just stop for a moment to break the cycle of chaos. Put on the brakes, even if it's only for five minutes. Maybe get a soda or water, top off your coffee or step outside for a minute. Take some time in your private moment to think, analyze or maybe even pray. Put some fresh thought into what the distraction really is. Ninety percent of the time the distraction will be familiar to us, and those feelings will rush into our mind's eye. Next, begin thinking about the boundaries we may need to draw to get the day under control. It may be to work in a conference room where you can have some privacy. Then search your task or "to-do" list for the item that is most important and urgent. Make it your primary focus in the moment. Maybe it's as easy as a follow-on call or an email you may need to deal with that has been eating at you. Take care of that first to get "the monkey off your back". Settle on *only* one or two top priorities for the remainder of the day. Choose the priority you know you can accomplish. When you complete it, you will feel like your day is back under control and you can tackle your next task with a vengeance.

Often, it won't always be as easy as described, but this is another tool to add to your tool belt for those tough days so you can feel like you added value to your work.

Finish Well

Excellence

"People forget how fast you did a job, but they remember how well you did it."

— *Howard W. Newton*

My wife, Laura, and I recently completed a community service project at a men's homeless shelter in Rochester, NY. Our scope was to redecorate a large community room/dining hall for the residents. The planned duration was four days, although the main project work took three very long working days. Honestly, it really was fun, eye opening, and a way to serve a challenged and ever-growing population. The overall objective was to help dignify these men in need who are currently down on their luck and in some cases desperate for help. The day we enjoyed the most was the closedown day — the fourth and final day. We felt this day had the greatest impact. For the "reveal" of their newly decorated room, we bought and served a pizza lunch, sodas and chocolate chip cookies to celebrate and honor these men and the staff. Laura and I observed the positive reactions around the room as everyone laughed and enjoyed the food. But mostly how they felt honored as we closed out the celebration and gave our final goodbyes. For us, the experience was quite a blessing and extremely rewarding!

Finish well! No matter the size of the project: big, small, long or short; whether at work, in our home, out in the yard or at a homeless shelter, the final outcome will always influence people. Leave no stone unturned and close down in a way that gives credibility to the project and to everyone that it impacts.

"I don't know about you, but I'm running hard for the finish line. I'm giving it everything I've got. No sloppy living for me!"

1 Corinthians 9:26 The Message

Excellence

Applied Project/Program Management

"Finish Well"

The *Project Management Body of Knowledge* (PMBOK®) talks specifically about activities we need to complete in order to close a project or project phase. Things like: making sure the work is done according to the requirements and any procurement closure, getting formal acceptance from the customer on the product of the project, assessing the performance of your team, archiving your project records, updating any historical or knowledge base you may have along with documenting lessons learned to pass along your final product, and lastly, releasing the resources. These are right out of the PMBOK®, and likely things we all know to do well to close a project and as part of the "science" of project management. But what about the "art" side at the close of a project? In our fast-paced "just in time", "no bench" corporate cultures, we often find PMs and team members having to scurry to find their next assignment, or even resources being prematurely yanked to another high-priority project. This ultimately leads to unfinished project closure, lost information, high-level stress, bad sentiment, and sometimes even resentment in the organization. Important

Certainly, there is no "one size fits all" solution to finishing a project or phase well, as this is an "art". Yet in the midst of closure here are a couple of thoughts that may serve you well:

- Be a "finish well" PM. Make it clear to the *current* sponsor of your project that you will not dash off to the next project without proper closure. Equally important, let the *next* project sponsor know that it is essential to the integrity of your project, your department and to honor the hard work of your team members that you need to make sure you close the project properly, just as you would for their project. People will honor your stand — in almost every case. There may be a short time of overlap between two projects, but if you have set this expectation, it will serve you well.

- In addition, set the same expectation of your team. Communicate your stand on project closure. Be clear about their involvement and be sure to get their buy-in, work hard to get them placed in their next project.

Chapter 9

Rewards and Recognition

Working with a Passion

Rewards and Recognition

"...the greatest asset I possess, and the way to develop the best that is in a person is by appreciation and encouragement."

— Charles Schwab

I have always been a big proponent of recognition. I believe it honors people that truly deserve to be recognized for work well done or for going above and beyond to complete a task or activity. With that said, I have also been in many spirited conversations on this topic, as many believe it should be the primary motivator toward a successful end result. Certainly for some, I have seen the impact.

However, I think many recognition plans may have it backward. Motivation should be self-induced. Meaning that as practicing leaders, we should find ourselves motivated by the passions that generate excitement inwardly so we can demonstrate this outwardly to our teams. I admit it; I like it when my leader or even my team notices or recognizes work well done. Yet receiving recognition should not be an expectation we desire as our primary motivator. However, it should be a validation that our passion is driving us in a successful direction for the good of the project and/or the organization.

"Moses inspected the work and saw that they had done it just as the Lord had commanded. So Moses blessed them."

Exodus 39:43 NIV

Rewards and Recognition

Applied Program/Project Leadership

"Working with Passion"

I believe each project/program should develop and execute a recognition plan as one part of their planning process deliverables. This is often left undone, as many desire to develop that plan on the fly.

The rub for me is that recognition is often used by project/program managers as "something that serves to induce or influence" which, in fact, is Webster's definition of a *bribe*! Is that really our intention? Recognition is our opportunity to reward and motivate both individuals and teams for work well done and for going above and beyond expectations. We want to give back to those talented people that display a red-hot passion for their work and accomplishments.

When we develop a recognition plan for projects/programs, we must work diligently to match up team members in their area(s) of passion and interest first. One way to do this is to simply ask what motivates them and what they are interested in doing. Get excited for them then pause and listen. Get "big ears" for what they have to say. Hear what jazzes them and work hard to connect them to those activities that will serve as their own internal tool for motivation. Let them know the vision of your project/program. Share your thoughts with them on how you plan to challenge and stretch their capability. Then value their contribution. This will foster project/program buy-in and enthusiasm beyond your expectations.

A Blind Eye

Rewards and Recognition

"Appreciation is a wonderful thing. It makes what is excellent in others belong to us as well."

— Voltaire

As leaders, we can sometimes go through our day with blinders on and not even know it. Meaning that all those good things that go on all around us even in the midst of chaos we just don't even see. Maybe we are too close to it, or we just aren't paying as much attention as we should be.

We must not be blind to the value our team members bring to bear. It is so easy to get used to a competent, high-performance team. We can be blind to their successes and never acknowledge how well they actually perform. This is very dishonoring to them.

Let's all remember to take off our blinders and remain alert. Tune in, observe, listen, and honor your team members at every opportunity. They deserve it!

"Love each other with genuine affection, and take delight in honoring each other. "

Romans 12:10 NLT

Rewards and Recognition

Applied Project/Program Management

"A Blind Eye"

Our leadership role requires us to have an overarching view of the *entire* project/program. When our projects/programs are humming along nicely, it is easy to ignore the areas that need a little extra thought-leadership, oversight or action.

As leaders we must multitask. We have to so we can survive. Inevitably, we gravitate to those areas that come naturally to us, but in the heat of the moment this can create a blind spot. This blind spot may result in being unprepared for a meeting, a late project deliverable, or more importantly a missed opportunity to honor someone on our team for a project accomplishment.

We can all agree that each of us has strengths and weaknesses we must contend with. No one expects us to know it all and be the best at everything all the time — none of us can be. But one area where we can't have a blind eye is understanding and recognizing the strengths, weaknesses and areas of passion of each of our team members.

Our role is to find ways to leverage the areas of strengths and passion of each of our team members — assuming we want the best chance at a successful project/program with a motivated team. Assigning roles to our teams that play to their strengths and passions will unlock potential we may not have seen before.

You might be pleasantly surprised how an unsuspecting team member may desire to lead your change control board or want to be a risk manager/coordinator or risk owner. You may find someone that loves metrics or has an in-depth knowledge of configuration management.

If you match their passion to position, acknowledge and reward each person's success, and coach them through their challenges along the way, your team and your project will be successful. The bonus is they *may* even enjoy doing it. Oh the *joy* of leading a motivated team!

Whole = Sum of its Parts

Rewards and Recognition

"You need to be aware of what others are doing, applaud their efforts, acknowledge their successes, and encourage them in their pursuits. When we all help one another, everybody wins."

— *Jim Stovall*

In our challenging work environment, both public and private victories don't seem to come our way very often. We may find ourselves *never* being content with the fruit of our labors. Typically most will celebrate those big wins as they come. But I encourage you to shift your paradigm.

Consider even a small win as a victory and celebrate those as well. Let's begin thinking in terms of setting ourselves up for smaller more frequent successes both in planning and in practice so as a team we can enjoy both.

When we experience the success of short-term victories, we gain momentum to yield more long-term successes, one step at a time.

"Do not withhold good from those who deserve it when it's in your power to help them."

Proverbs 3:27 NLT

Rewards and Recognition

Applied Project/Program Management

"Whole = Sum of its Parts"

Consider success measures when developing your start-up activities to create a high-impact planning phase. Often we trap ourselves or facilitate looking too far down the road at just the big milestones such as completing a big deliverable like our scope statement, design specifications, or delivering a finished requirements document. Make no mistake, documentation milestones like these are critical, but many times we reach so far forward that we may lose sight of the smaller victories that bring us closer to begin with. These small victories along the path toward bigger deliverables may seem trivial to some but never to those who are in the thick of it. We must leverage these times of positive momentum for motivation and encouragement for our team.

Consider taking time to plan and recognize important, *not just the urgent*, completed activities or work packages. Maybe a team member completed four sections of the first draft of your scope document or one may be drafting the first seven critical requirements, and both are done extremely well. It could be a key team member who identified two risk opportunities and created a mitigation plan to potentially *save* the project money. Consider something less tangible, like when a team member volunteers a few extra hours to complete an activity for another teammate who is out ill.

When project/program managers recognize these smaller, completed victories on a regular basis, this will generate a team leadership model that will cascade throughout our project/programs and undoubtedly create momentum and excitement for your team.

Remember this important formula: the Whole = the sum of its parts.

Chapter 10

Growth

Professional Growth

Growth

"You must have an aim; a vision; a goal. The person sailing through life with no destination or 'port-of- call', every wind is the wrong wind."

— Tracy Brinkmann, Success Counselor

I thank God for my job as well as the consulting and teaching work that I do part time. I need to pray more prayers of thanks for this blessing. Maybe like you, I too have had times when I have been out of work and searching for a new job.

Recently, I finished a three-month semester of teaching a ten-week Project Management Professional Certification Exam Prep course. At the close of the last class, I challenged the learners to think about this question: "What is it that differentiates you and me as professionals from everyone else? What is the uniqueness that you or I bring to the table?"

I often ask myself, what is it that drives me to work hard and add the greatest value to my workplace/employer?

I have asked this question many times of other professionals, and even my children as they grow into their professional lives. Now I challenge you to think about this in your own mind's eye. So here it is:

Start with this sobering thought. There is always someone better, smarter or more skilled than you or me. With that said, take a moment next time you are at work to look at the door in your office or cubical. Visualize a long line of people standing at your doorway. They are people that may already be unemployed, co-workers, or maybe people from other companies that would love, even crave, to have your job. Maybe they are smarter or more skilled than you. Ask yourself what makes you or me a better choice for our employer. What do we have over those in that imaginary, long line at your door just waiting to sit in your chair?

I believe it is *not* simply our right to have a job, it is more of a privilege that we have worked hard to earn. We *must* be passionate to differentiate ourselves from others if we want to hang on to what we have, or to move onto the next opportunity.

I encourage you to enhance your professional credibility by working hard to differentiate yourself.

Create a long-term plan to span over the course of one or maybe two years. Begin with a self-analysis revolving around this question: "What really jazzes me?"

I have found coaching, mentoring and teaching the project management discipline to be an area that truly jazzes me. Over the last several years, I have worked hard through these simple yet critical steps to have a significant, positive impact and influence on those I have served.

Don't delay — start your plan today!

- Determine how much effort you can dedicate.
- Take some time to decide on your specific goals for your first year. Make your goals achievable yet challenging.
- Develop an action plan, schedule and measures. **Tip: Don't over-think or obsess on these.**
- Add milestones for times of celebration when you complete a goal or even an action.
- Stick to your plan but cut yourself some slack for those crazy days when life overwhelms you. Then recover and get back on track.

You won't be sorry you did!

"The plans of the diligent lead to profit as surely as haste leads to poverty."

Proverbs 21:5 NIV

Re-invent Yourself
Growth

"Those people who develop the ability to continuously acquire new and better forms of knowledge that they can apply to their work and to their lives will be the movers and shakers in our society for the indefinite future."

— Brian Tracy

In order for businesses to stay alive in a competitive global market, we find companies leveraging their fundamental success and then re-inventing it. Campbell's® Soup, popular for their condensed soup, have added many new products to their line like the popular Campbell's® Chunky Soups or Campbell's® Kids Soups, all with redesigned packaging and pop-off tops. How about 3M's invention of Post-it® Notes in the 1970's? Now the Post-it Note brand has an entire product line. You can buy Post-it Note flags, dispensers, easel pads even pens with Post-it Notes. The product list goes on and on with enumerable shapes, sizes and colors.

In a similar sense, in today's complex business environment, leaders need to leverage their fundamental knowledge but always be open to new innovative ways of leading. Gone are the days of the "one size fits all" management style. We should be well read and attend seminars and workshops. We should step outside of our comfort zone and take calculated risks that come with new learning and innovative leading. Don't get stuck in the "old-school" mentality, it could make a huge difference in your growing your career.

"Observe people who are good at their work — skilled workers are always in demand and admired; they don't take a backseat to anyone."

Proverbs 22:29 The Message

Growth

Applied Project/Program Management

"Re-invent Yourself"

People that know me will tell you I am a big believer in executing the fundamentals flawlessly. In my days of coaching my son's teams, my mantra was to first make sure athletes had solid fundamental skills. Even as they excelled in sports as young boys and now into their careers, newer, more innovative skills have followed in their growth and maturity. Yet my boys will tell you we talk from time to time about the importance of doing the fundamental things right.

Project/program managers are no different, as we must be grounded in the fundamental practices of the PM disciplines. Yet as maturing leaders we become more skillful and apply more complex tactics to help us re-invent ourselves. Application of more mature skills and strategies must be appropriate and commensurate to the breadth and depth of your project. Meaning: don't do something for the sake of just doing it. If it doesn't have measurable value, stop doing it.

With that said, keep these four pieces of knowledge in the forefront as you manage projects:

- Change it up! Don't be mundane. If you need a different kind of meeting to collect status, then make the change. Check out Pat Lencioni's book *Death by Meetings*.
- Keep it simple! It is very easy to get wrapped up in the complexity, so tone it down.
- Use "why" as a tool. Meaning that if you are going to apply a new practice, tactic, skill or measure to your project, know and be able to articulate why you are using it and the value it brings.
- Make it about your customer. This is the most obvious. For every action you take and decision you make, consider the impact to the customer and/or the user.

Applying these fundamental learning's along with new techniques can influence how you make your future project/program decisions and could be the difference between success and failure.

Learning While You Lead
Growth

"An investment in knowledge always pays the best interest."
— *Benjamin Franklin*

Over a hundred years ago people were typically paid for their labor — physical labor. The role of the manager was to improve how people carried out those physical tasks. In some regard this is true today, but by most standards, mid-level managers are paid to think. Our brains create order out of chaos, making links between information so our lives make more sense. It is like having a new piece of software, initially we are a bit confused at the shortcuts, but once we learn them, it becomes a breeze. The same is true as we develop our leadership skills. When we process complex thoughts, we tap into our visual centers and ideas flash into our mind's eye, and we have what some would call an "aha!" moment. When those ideas that were not linked before come together, it feels like a new idea, and there is an actual chemical release into our body. That chemical release creates our motivation to act. Habits are created and those habits create your experiences.

Learning while leading comes in various forms, and we must never stop our learning process. One extraordinary way is learning from our team. Seek it out, soak it up, and add it to our leadership toolbox.

"Intelligent people are always ready to learn. Their ears are open for knowledge."

Proverbs 18:15 NLT

Growth

Applied Project/Program Management

"Learning While You Lead"

The PM discipline can bring the pieces of a project puzzle together, juggle the priorities, and we can experience an outcome that is honoring to the team, ourselves, and to our employer.

But it never fails, in every project/program, we run into those circumstances with resources, project anomalies, and/or situations we may never have seen before. This is not an uncommon phenomenon in our jobs or life itself, thus a new learning opportunity comes along.

Learning comes in many shapes and sizes, and we should never tire of it. In my experience, I have found many lessons learned from individuals on my project team. Great solutions to really tough problems are often solved by getting our amazing team members into the mix. Even in the most critical times when the wheels seem to be to falling off, we need to be in tune with those unsuspecting teammates to build creative solutions we may have never thought of on our own. Each member is unique and they bring their experiences into the mix. All we need to do is seek it out. Watch what happens and you'll see how each individual rises to the occasion. Don't be surprised how willing they are to contribute. Surely we can make a good decision together.

Like most leaders, we want a great decision, so let's get out of our own way and call on our project team, who will make or break our project success.

Success to Significance

Growth

"Vision without action is merely a dream. Action without vision just passes the time. Vision with action can change the world!"

— Joel Barker

Do you have a compass or roadmap for your professional and, more importantly, your personal life? Most seem to develop a career mission, objectives, and even a long-term plan toward career success. Yet many of us don't carry that practice over to our personal lives. We fail to develop a personal life mission and long-term life plan toward personal significance.

Find some time to reflect and do some soul searching. If you have ever wanted to give to the less fortunate or volunteer at a homeless shelter, and even had a desire to be a better friend, maybe now is the time to make that commitment.

Build your personal life roadmap, then follow your compass and stay true north.

"Where there is no vision, the people are unrestrained."
Proverbs 29:18 NASB

Growth

Applied Project/Program Leadership

"Success to Significance"

You won't find this in the *Project Management Body of Knowledge* (PMBOK®), but it has served me well. The unspoken reality is that although on time and on budget is the desired norm for most for project success, significance is the differentiator. Meaning that long term we want our sponsor, team, and stakeholders to see the significance of our project based on its success. Don't be confused that projects by definition have a definite start and end date. However, what the project delivers can have long-term effects and influence over the long haul.

Create a vision and/or mission in your projects/programs. People need a roadmap, a destination so they not only know where they are headed but why. I have found that team members are more positive when they have a sense of where they are going.

Start by sketching out your vision/mission, but don't over-think it. Use this to get you started:

<u>Vision Statement</u>: Vision is a short, succinct, and inspiring statement of what the project/program intends to become and to achieve at some point in the future. It should resonate with all members of the team and help them feel proud, excited, and part of something much bigger than themselves.

<u>Mission Statement</u>: A statement of the role, or purpose, by which a project/program intends to serve its stakeholders. This describes what the project/program does (current capabilities), who it serves (stakeholders), and what makes the project/program unique (justification for existence).

<u>Next</u>: Share it with your team and let them contribute as a team before you finalize it. Take their feedback away and finalize it.

This will create a sense of team synergy and buy-in.

Annual Physical

Growth

"The longer I live the less confidence I have in drugs and the greater is my confidence in the regulation and administration of diet and regimen."

— John Redman Coxe, 1800

I had my annual physical late on a Friday afternoon. I really like my doctor, but I don't enjoy *going* to the doctor. And to top it off, this year I brought along a list. (By the way, it was my wife who generated the list.) I am a young fifty-year-old male at the midpoint of my life. I have a few aches and pains maybe just like you, but overall I feel great. I do have a few things to work on to maintain a well-balanced and healthy lifestyle. I am trying to shed a few pounds, stay active, eat well and exercise.

What I am getting at is a brief word on watching oneself. Simply a heartfelt note for us to take care of our health, as our health is everything. It doesn't matter what age we are, but it makes all the difference for our quality of life. How we manage our personal life impacts who we are and what we do. Ours choices will make all the difference in how we perform at work and enable us to get through our day-to-day activities with ease, confidence and alertness.

Just like planning and executing a long-term project, while leading our team we need to meet some critical health-related milestones to be successful in the long-term.

So in my research, I found some helpful wisdom from **WebMD** that I'd like to pass along to you:

- *Don't Skip Breakfast*: by Kelli Miller Stacy, *WebMD Health News*, Reviewed by Louise Chang, MD — "Skipping breakfast is often a big no-no if you are trying to lose or maintain weight because it leads to high-calorie cravings later."

- *Eating Out*: by Sheila Cohn, RD, a spokesperson for the *National Restaurant Association* — "Good choices consist of meals that have lots of fruits and veggies, lean fish or chicken, lean cuts of meat, veggie-based sauces instead of cream sauces — there are always healthy options on every restaurant menu."

- *Start Adding Veggies*: by Rick Hall, RD, of Phoenix — "When you are building a sandwich, choose high amounts of veggies, like tomatoes, cucumbers, green peppers, and red peppers, which add a lot of nutrients."

- *Fast Food*: by Elaine Magee, MPH, *WebMD Weight Loss Clinic* — "If you go to a typical fast-food burger place, opt for the charbroiled chicken sandwich without creamy sauce (ask for BBQ sauce, catsup, or mustard) or a small hamburger without mayo or special sauce. This next step is going to hurt: Instead of fries, reach for a salad with a low-fat dressing or a fruit salad. If fries are non-negotiable, get the kiddies size and just enjoy some of them."

- *Exercise*: by Virginia Anderson, *WebMD Feature* and Reviewed by Louise Chang, MD — "So we all know exercise is good for us. Don't start off trying to work out an hour every day. Instead, begin with 20-30 minutes of your chosen exercise two to three times a week. It's essential to find an activity you like... Don't let previous bad experiences with exercise hinder you."

- *More Exercise*: by Miranda Hitti, *WebMD Health News*, Reviewed by Brunilda Nazario, MD — "Don't let brain chatter talk you out of exercise and don't give your brain time to hem and haw about it."

- *Bad Mood Busters*: by *WebMD's Editorial Staff* — "Exercise, changing your diet, and even playing with a pet can help improve your mood. There's a connection between mind and body. A healthy diet not only fuels your body, but it also helps you feel better... Choose exercise you enjoy. Just take a walk with a friend. As time goes on, increase activity until you exercise on most days... You'll feel better physically and sleep better at night. Staying connected with other people helps overcome the lethargy, exhaustion, and loneliness... Learning to mentally relax can help restore a sense of calm and control... you could simply listen to soothing music while you take a long, hot bath. Call a friend and go for a walk. Have a cup of coffee with your partner."

- *Get the Rest You Need*: by *WebMD's Editorial Staff* — "Start by going to bed and getting up the same time each day. Use relaxation techniques to help fall asleep. Healthy sleep makes you feel better physically and mentally."

- *Stress Management*: by *WebMD's Editorial Staff* — "Stress is a fact of life. Although some stress is normal and even needed, too much of it can affect your quality of life and your health. People who don't manage stress well can have headaches, stomach pain, sleeping problems, illness, and depression. You can manage stress by journaling, meditating, exercising, talking to others, or engaging in a hobby."

- *More Stress Management*: by *WebMD's Editorial Staff* — "When you feel stressed, you can: Take slow, deep breaths. Soak in a warm bath. Listen to soothing music. Take a walk or do some other activity. Meditate or pray. Take a yoga class. Have a massage or back rub. Have a warm drink that doesn't have alcohol or caffeine."

Thanks for taking time to review and consider a few tips on maintaining your health to increase your overall quality of life. Take some time to research areas more specific to your needs at: http://www.webmd.com/.

"...You are not your own; you were bought at a price. Therefore honor God with your body."

1 Corinthians 6:19-20 (NIV)

Growth

Applied Project/Program Leadership

"Annual Physical"

We know for sure our projects suffer their own aches and pains throughout the project lifecycle. What better way to keep them healthy than checking each for their overall project health? It is like a project physical except we need to be looking at our projects more frequently than just once a year.

There are many ways projects and programs can be checked for good health. Some may consider an on-time, on-budget measure for the health of a project. Certainly this will tell us if the project is on time and/or on budget, but does this really measure the health of the project as a whole? I want to dig down one step deeper and separate the Project/Program Health Check as its own entity.

There are multiple definitions to what some would see as a Project Health Check:

...to measure process maturity

...to detect problems early

...to identify factors that will enable or disable the outcome of a project

One would suggest this is used because we don't want any surprises.

All of these thoughts certainly have relevance, but your organization must determine what works best and then implement a Project Health Check based on the value and need.

It is extremely easy for projects to "hide" issues that may not be obvious on the surface. Therefore, it is important to make sure you consider ways of detecting project problems early on so your project team has the ability to deal with them. A Health Check could be viewed as a snapshot at a certain point in time. Different to a status meeting, a Health Check can assist your project to improve performance or even turn a deteriorating project around. In essence, a Project Health Check is a scheduled project event designed to assess the project's overall situation. It will assist in satisfaction of customers/users and provide relevant feedback and recommendations toward the positive health of a project. It can also serve as a tool for immediate action plans toward project recovery. Finally, consider this Health Check activity as a team-building event. Remember, Health Checks are designed to *HELP* your projects if they are in trouble or reassure your teams, stakeholders and customers that all is well. A Project Health Check is NOT as a tool to drive down project managers and teams.

I would encourage you to consider conducting project or program Health Checks quarterly or at least biannually.

I thought I would make a couple of suggestions that have been effective in many projects where I have been involved. However, consider what is most important in your own organization, and do your research. There are many tools out there that can make this activity quite easy to execute as well as the ability to customize the process to your own needs. Consider using a simple survey to collect project information in some critical areas. Here are some suggested areas you may want to consider.

Scope Management is ensuring that the project completes all the work identified and approved, no more or no less. Ask in a short survey if the requirements are clearly written, reviewed and executed.

- Have we completed a well-developed work breakdown structure?
- Has a change control process been built, implemented and effective?
- Have we included the appropriate stakeholders in managing and communicating scope progress and/or changes?

Communication Management closes the communication divide between stakeholders involved with the project. Ask if there is a positive relationship with our primary stakeholders and if this project has a strong team dynamic.

- Do you have and execute the communication plan effectively?
- Do you execute internal and external status meetings?
- Is your project sponsor engaged and aware of your project progress?

Risk Management is the ability to increase probability and impact of the project's positive events and decrease the probability and impact of the project's negative events. Ask if your Risk Management plan is in place.

- Is the project team executing and managing it?
- Have you identified risks and do you have them documented?
- Are there risk owners?
- Do you have handling plans for the high-impact risks?
- Do you regularly monitor and control risks collected?

Schedule Management leverages your WBS to develop your schedule activities.

- Did you confer with your team before finalizing the estimated time for each activity?
- Do you have a process to include communications when making changes in your schedule?
- Are you measuring schedule progress needed throughout the project process?

Human Resource Management incorporates those processes that organize, manage and foster leadership of the project team.

- Are you managing your resources based on your HR Management Plan?
- Have you clearly articulated the roles and responsibilities of everyone to all project team members?
- Are your team members aware of the recognition plan, and is it being executed?
- Are you working to match resources with their strengths toward growth?

Quality Management must satisfy those needs of the project for which it was undertaken. Consider asking:

- Is the project managing against it baselines (schedule, cost, time, scope)?
- Are we collecting and reporting metrics based on the measurement plan?
- Has a QA Plan been developed, and is it being executed?
- Are we conducting quality audits as planned?

This list is not an all-inclusive list, but it does represent some of the most critical areas of our projects. If regular Health Checks (quarterly, biannually) are executed by an unbiased, supportive representative or group (project or program office), you can expect much cleaner projects from start to finish. I encourage you to consider utilizing Project Health Checks for overall project health.

Quote References

Quote References

"Honesty is the first chapter in the book of wisdom."

— *Thomas Jefferson*

"If you truly know and care for the people entrusted to your leadership, they will instinctively take care of the mission, one another and their leader. But none of this will be possible until you know your people."

— *Commentary by Capt. Marcos Baca 386th Expeditionary Force Support Squadron Deputy Commander United States Air Force.*

"The key to successful leadership is influence, not authority."

— *Ken Blanchard*

"It is literally true that you can succeed best and quickest by helping others to succeed."

— *Napoleon Hill, 1883-1970*

"The one unchangeable certainly is that nothing is unchangeable or certain."

— *John F. Kennedy*

"...the greatest asset I possess, and the way to develop the best that is in a person is by appreciation and encouragement."

— *Charles Schwab*

"The next step in building a dream team is to establish clear criterion for the selection of specific team members. Character. Competence. Chemistry."

— *Bill Hybels*

"To forgive is to set a prisoner free and discover that the prisoner was you."

— *Lewis B. Smedes*

"It was pride that changed angels into devils; it is humility that makes men as angels."

— *Saint Augustine*

"You must have an aim; a vision; a goal. The person sailing through life with no destination or 'port-of- call', every wind is the wrong wind."

— *Tracy Brinkmann, Success Counselor*

"Example is not the main thing in influencing others. It is the only thing."

— *Albert Schweitzer*

"At times, it is difficult to keep a proper balance in our lives. But, over time, an improper balance will lead to problems."

— *Catherine Pulsifer*

"The BusyLeader must take time to look for God's direction and then act on it."

— Pat Richie

"Every now and then go away, have a little relaxation, for when you come back to your work your judgment will be surer."

— *Leonardo Da Vinci*

"Practice Golden-Rule 1 of Management in everything you do. Manage others the way you would like to be managed."

— *Brian Tracy*

"Vision without action is merely a dream. Action without vision just passes the time. Vision with action can change the world!"

— *Joel Barker*

"Leadership rests not only upon ability, not only upon capacity; having the capacity to lead is not enough. The leader must be willing to use it. His leadership is then based on truth and character. There must be truth in the purpose and will power in the character."

— *Vince Lombardi*

"Attitude is a little thing that makes a big difference."

— *Winston Churchill*

"Seek first to understand, then to be understood."

— *St. Francis of Assisi*

"To know you have enough is to be rich."

— *Lao-Tzu, Tao Te Ching*

"Our greatest problem is not the mistakes we make in life, but that we fail to learn from them."

— *Chuck Swindoll*

"In life, what you resist, persists."

— *Werner Erhard*

Quote References

"It's more important as a manager to be respected than to be popular."

— *Ken Blanchard & Don Shula*

"Only by contending with challenges that seem to be beyond your strength to handle at the moment can you grow more surely toward the stars."

— *Brian Tracy*

"I do the very best I know how, the very best I can, and I mean to keep on doing so until the end."

— *Abraham Lincoln*

"Good habits result from resisting temptation."

— *Ancient Proverb*

"When it comes to life the critical thing is whether you take things for granted or take them with gratitude."

— *G. K. Chesterton*

"Appreciation is a wonderful thing. It makes what is excellent in others belong to us as well."

— *Voltaire*

"You must master your time rather than becoming a slave to the constant flow of events and demands on your time. And you must organize your life to achieve balance, harmony, and inner peace."

— *Brian Tracy*

"Wisdom is the reward you get for a lifetime of listening when you'd have preferred to talk."

— *Doug Larson*

"Our work is the presentation of our capabilities."

— *Johann Wolfgang Von Goethe*

"You need to be aware of what others are doing, applaud their efforts, acknowledge their successes, and encourage them in their pursuits. When we all help one another, everybody wins."

— *Jim Stovall*

"If what you're seeking is lasting relationships, long-term success and quality of life in all areas then you will be better served to forego the pompous acts of the arrogant for the humility and quiet confidence displayed by true leaders."

— *Unknown*

"Those people who develop the ability to continuously acquire new and better forms of knowledge that they can apply to their work and to their lives will be the movers and shakers in our society for the indefinite future."

— *Brian Tracy*

"I found that the men and women who got to the top were those who did the jobs they had in hand, with everything they had of energy and enthusiasm and hard work."

— *Harry S. Truman*

"Catch on fire with enthusiasm and people will come from miles to watch you burn."

— *John Wesley*

"The most important single ingredient in the formula of success is knowing how to get along with people."

— *Theodore Roosevelt*

"Don't wait for people to be friendly, show them how."

— *Unknown*

"Interdependent people combine their own efforts with the efforts of others to achieve their greatest success."

— *Stephen Covey*

"A leader, once convinced that a particular course of action is the right one, must be undaunted when the going gets tough."

— *Ronald Reagan*

"Those who are blessed with the most talent don't necessarily outperform everyone else. It's the people with follow-through who excel."

— *Mary Kay Ash*

"If there is any great secret of success in life, it lies in the ability to put yourself in the other person's place and to see things from his point of view – as well as your own."

— *Henry Ford*

"Balance, peace, and joy are the fruit of a successful life. It starts with recognizing your talents and finding ways to serve others by using them."

— *Thomas Kinkade*

Quote References

"By the power of faith every enduring work is accomplished."

— *James Allen*

"People forget how fast you did a job, but they remember how well you did it."

— *Howard W. Newton*

"Live a balanced life - learn some and think some and draw and paint and sing and dance and play and work every day some."

— *Robert Fulghum*

"Treat people as if they were what they ought to be and you help them to become what they are capable of being."

— *Johann Wolfgang von Goethe*

"An investment in knowledge always pays the best interest."

— *Benjamin Franklin*

"They don't care how much you know until they know how much you care."

— *John C. Maxwell*

"Vision is knowing who are you, where you're going and what will guide your journey."

— *Ken Blanchard and Jesse Stoner*

"You need to be aware of what others are doing, applaud their efforts, acknowledge their successes, and encourage them in their pursuits. When we all help one another, everybody wins."

— *Jim Stovall*

"Having a simple, clearly defined goal can capture the imagination and inspire passion. It can cut through the fog like a beacon in the night."

— *Unknown*

"The ultimate measure of a person is not where they stand in moments of comfort and convenience, but where the stand in times of challenge and controversy."

— *Martin Luther King, Jr.*

"Servant-leadership encourages collaboration, trust, foresight, listening, and the ethical use of power and empowerment"

— *Letze Oostinga, MA MGM*

"We seek the truth and will endure the consequences."

— *Charles Seymour*

"The longer I live the less confidence I have in drugs and the greater is my confidence in the regulation and administration of diet and regimen."

— **John Redman Coxe, 1800**

Bible References

"So be strong and courageous! Do not be afraid and do not panic before them. For the Lord your God will personally go ahead of you. He will neither fail you nor abandon you."

Deuteronomy 31:6 NLT

"A generous man will prosper; he who refreshes others will himself be refreshed."

Proverbs 11:25 NIV

"Give me an understanding heart so that I can govern your people well and know the difference between right and wrong. For who by himself is able to govern this great people of yours?"

1 Kings 3:9 NLT

"My son, preserve sound judgment and discernment, do not let them out of your sight;"

Proverbs 3:21 NIV

"But as for you, be strong and do not give up, for your work will be rewarded."

2 Chronicles 15:7 NIV

"Plans go wrong for lack of advice; many advisers bring success."

Proverbs 15:22

"I've commanded you to be strong and brave. Don't ever be afraid or discouraged! I am the LORD your God, and I will be there to help you wherever you go."

Joshua 1:9 CEV

"There is a time to cry and a time to laugh. There is a time to be sad and a time to dance."

Ecclesiastes 3:4 NCV

"As iron sharpens iron, so people can improve each other."

Proverbs 27:17 (NCV)

"In this world the kings and great men order their people around, and yet they are called 'friends of the people.' But among you, those who are the greatest should take the lowest rank, and the leader should be like a servant."

Luke 22:25-26 NLT

"Walk in wisdom toward outsiders, making the best use of the time. Let your speech always be gracious, seasoned with salt, so that you may know how you ought to answer each person."

Colossians 4:5-6 ESV

"Care for the flock that God has entrusted to you. Watch over it willingly, not grudgingly—not for what you will get out of it, but because you are eager to serve God. Don't lord it over the people assigned to your care, but lead them by your own good example. And when the Great Shepherd appears, you will receive a crown of never-ending glory and honor."

1 Peter 5:2-4 NLT

"Instead, speaking the truth in love, we will in all things grow up into him who is the Head, that is, Christ."

Ephesians 4:15 (NIV)

"For I can do everything through Christ, who gives me strength."

Philippians 4:13 NLT

"Pride comes before destruction, and an arrogant spirit before a fall."

Proverbs 16:18 (HCSB)

"For those who exalt themselves will be humbled, and those who humble themselves will be exalted."

Luke 18:14 NLT

"Then Peter came to him and asked, "Lord, how often should I forgive someone who sins against me? Seven times? No, not seven times, Jesus replied, but seventy times seven!"

Mathew 18:21-22 NLT

"Let all that I am praise the Lord; may I never forget the good things he does for me."

Psalm 103:2 NLT

"Consider it a sheer gift, friends, when tests and challenges come at you from all sides. You know that under pressure, your faith-life is forced into the open and shows its true colors. So don't try to get out of anything prematurely. Let it do its work so you become mature and well-developed, not deficient in any way."

James 1:2-4 The Message

Bible References

"Now then, my sons, listen to me and do not depart from the words of my mouth."

Proverbs 5:7 NASB

"For the Lord grants wisdom! From his mouth come knowledge and understanding."

Proverbs 2:6 NLT

"For the Lord gives wisdom, and from His mouth come knowledge and understanding."

Proverbs 3:13 NIV

"Blessed are those who act justly, who always do what is right."

Psalm 106:3 TNIV

"The wise in heart are called discerning, and gracious words promote instruction."

Proverbs 16:21 TNIV

"No discipline is enjoyable while it is happening—it's painful! But afterward there will be a peaceful harvest of right living for those who are trained in this way."

Hebrews 12:11 HCSB

"Careless words stab like a sword, but wise words bring healing."

Proverbs 12:18 NCV

"After the apostles returned to Jesus, they told him everything they had done and taught. But so many people were coming and going that Jesus and the apostles did not even have a chance to eat. Then Jesus said, "Let's go to a place where we can be alone and get some rest."

Mark 6:30-31 CEV

"For in six days the Lord made heaven and earth, but he rested on the seventh day and was refreshed."

Exodus 31:17 NLT

"There's an opportune time to do things, a right time for everything on the earth."

Ecclesiastes 3:1 The Message

"It is useless for you to work so hard from early morning until late at night, anxiously working for food to eat; for God gives rest to his loved ones."

Psalm 127:2 NLT

"I have seen what is best for people here on earth. They should eat and drink and enjoy their work, because the life God has given them on earth is short."

Ecclesiastes 5:18 NCV

"They must first be tested; and then if there is nothing against them, let them serve as deacons."

1 Timothy 3:10 TNIV

"And whatever you do or say, do it as a representative of the Lord Jesus, giving thanks through him to God the Father."

Colossians 3:17 NLT

"I am the good shepherd; I know my sheep and my sheep know me."

John 10:14 TNIV

"Rich people may think they are wise, but a poor person with discernment can see right through them."

Proverbs 28:11 NLT

"Happy is the man who doesn't give in and do wrong when he is tempted, for afterwards he will get as his reward the crown of life that God has promised those who love Him."

James 1:12 TLB

"In the end, people appreciate honest criticism far more than flattery."

Proverbs 28:23 NLT

"Always be humble and gentle. Be patient with each other, making allowance for each other's faults because of your love. Make every effort to keep yourselves united in the Spirit, binding yourselves together with peace."

Ephesians 4:2-3 NLT

"And let us be concerned about one another in order to promote love and good works."

Hebrews 10:24 HCSB

"Finally, brothers and sisters, rejoice! Strive for full restoration, encourage one another, be of one mind, live in peace. And the God of love and peace will be with you."

2 Corinthians 13:11 TNIV

BIBLE REFERENCES

"Therefore encourage one another and build each other up, just as in fact you are doing."

1 Thessalonians 5:11 NIV

"If a man makes a promise to the Lord or says he will do something special, he must keep his promise. He must do what he said."

Numbers 30:2 NCV

"In all the work you are doing, work the best you can. Work as if you were doing it for the Lord, not for people."

Colossians 3:23 NCV

"Work hard so you can present yourself to God and receive his approval."

2 Timothy 2:15 NLT

"Whatever you do, do well. For when you go to the grave, there will be no work or planning or knowledge or wisdom."

Ecclesiastes 9:10 NLT

"I don't know about you, but I'm running hard for the finish line. I'm giving it everything I've got. No sloppy living for me!"

1 Corinthians 9:26 The Message

"Moses inspected the work and saw that they had done it just as the Lord had commanded. So Moses blessed them."

Exodus 39:43 NIV

"Love each other with genuine affection, and take delight in honoring each other."

Romans 12:10 NLT

"Do not withhold good from those who deserve it when it's in your power to help them."

Proverbs 3:27 NLT

"The plans of the diligent lead to profit as surely as haste leads to poverty."

Proverbs 21:5 NIV

"Observe people who are good at their work— skilled workers are always in demand and admired; they don't take a backseat to anyone."

Proverbs 22:29 The Message

"Intelligent people are always ready to learn. Their ears are open for knowledge."

Proverbs 18:15 NLT

"Where there is no vision, the people are unrestrained."

Proverbs 29:18 NASB

"...You are not your own; you were bought at a price. Therefore honor God with your body."

1 Corinthians 6:19-20 (NIV)

About the Author

STEVEN WILSON has two decades of experience in project and program management. He is currently employed with a leading global technology services company. He has consulted to senior leaders and leadership teams in organizations ranging from Fortune 500 companies and start-ups to churches and non-profits. Steve is also Vice President and co-founder of Journey Consulting, specializing in project management and leadership training, coaching and consulting for organizations, and PMI® Chapters. Steve is the Principal Consultant and Lead Instructor on leadership, project management and team dynamics.

After receiving his PMP® Certification in 2003, Steve has successfully developed and delivered PMP® Certification Exam Prep training to more then five hundred PMs in the US, Canada, Argentina, Mexico and the UK. Ninety-eight percent of those who sit for the PMP® Exam have passed and are now certified project management professionals.

In addition to training and consulting, Steve is a sought-after speaker on topics relating to leadership and the tactical and strategic areas of project management.

Steve holds a Bachelor and Master of Science in Education and worked as a professional educator for fourteen years.

Steve lives with his wife, Laura, in Fairport, New York. Steve has two grown sons, Peter and Timothy, who now live in LA and Buffalo respectively.

You can reach Steven at the Journey Consulting website, www.journeyconsulting.org or at swilson@journeyconsulting.org.